THE GREEN Songbook

42 Songs Arranged for Beginning Guitar

Jessica Anne Baron

GUITARS IN THE CLASSROOM

Alfred

Contents

Alfred Music Publishing Co., Inc.
P.O. Box 10003
Van Nuys, CA 91410-0003
alfred.com

ISBN-10: 0-7390-7121-1
ISBN-13: 978-0-7390-7121-2

 Alfred Cares. Contents printed on 100% recycled paper.

Welcome to
THE GREEN Songbook

I am proud to be a part of this songbook. Music is such a great way to bring people together; it has the ability to unite us. A song can help us communicate an idea to a child or help us travel to a place where we feel like a kid again ourselves. After years of visiting classrooms with my guitar I am always amazed with the energy of the students, their eagerness to sing-along, and the power that a song has to teach a lesson. If we want the next generation to be stewards of this earth, we need to help them grow a profound respect for nature…and then encourage them to sing out about it to the world.

Jack Johnson
musician

kōkua hawai'i foundation

The Green Songbook has been developed in part with generous support from the Johnson Ohana Charitable Foundation.

To receive more songs and information from Guitars in the Classroom, get up to date Green info, and to share your thoughts with other Green teachers and classrooms, please visit www.greensongbook.com.

We are so thankful...

Guitars in the Classroom (GITC) thanks everyone who contributed to this book from its inception to its completion! To GITC's Board of Directors' Billy Stern, Peter D'Addario, Dan Smith, Alisa Peres, and John Hawkins, our dedicated staff members Nick Sinutko and Debi Cavataio, and the numerous GITC instructors and classroom teachers who have contributed valuable content- thank you so much for your participation!

To Jack and Kim Johnson, and Jessica Scheeter of the Johnson Ohana Charitable Foundation, we extend evergreen gratitude to your generosity, guidance, and all-around support!

Thank you to the "book team," the "recording team," the "songwriting team," and each of our amazing contributors! Your brilliance, hard work, expertise, and generosity shine through these pages. We hope everyone will read about you in the back of the book.

To the Children's Music Network for helping Guitars in the Classroom reach out to the talented songwriters affiliated with their organization, a thousand thanks. One CMN member in particular, Nancy Schimmel, a woman who champions the cause of ecological sustainability and human kindness, spent hours guiding us to great songs and songwriters with like-minded dedication. You will find several of her songs in this collection. Thank you, Nancy.

To Guitars in the Classroom instructor Christopher Hills and his partner in love and life, Eva Brooks, thanks for joining us in creating the recordings—your talent, diligence, resources and supervision have been indispensable. To musicians Marie Gabrielle, Frank Christian, Julia Kim, and Jessica Finkelberg Silver, thank you for adding your talent, faith, and friendship to our efforts! To Linda Adrian for keeping the home fires burning in California while I was traveling to make this book, thank you so much. To Elias for patiently sharing your mom with an oversized workload, and for your enthusiasm for this project and for protecting our planet.

Guitars in the Classroom is exceptionally grateful to John Kiehl, Ric Schnupp, and Soundtrack Studio for contributing all the studio time and know-how to make our recordings music that can be shared in the classroom or living room and will double as a play-along practice CD for everyone learning to play these songs! John's inclusion of Guitars in the Classroom's work as part of an initiative at the United Nations to relieve human suffering through the creation of Millenium Development Goals utilizing Music As a Natural Resource will give Guitars in the Classroom's work, as well as this book, the opportunity to teach ecology and peace around the globe in the years ahead.

Guitars in the Classroom gives very special thanks to Thom Wolke, whose contributions to this project range from personally introducing GITC to many of this book's contributors, writers, songwriters, and session musicians; to singing in the studio with his precious daughters, and to creating the majority of the photos here. This book gives testimony to your creativity and determination to walk the walk and make this earth a better place for all of us and future generations.

The Green Songbook has been made very specially by Alfred Music Publishing, a company with the vision to go far above and beyond the norm to include songs of such great range and variety from the little-known to the world famous. Alfred's vision and charity allowed us to record a full length double CD set with complete versions of many of the songs in the book, and to create a song chart format that has never been done before! Alfred approved the use of Dick Boak's original artwork for our cover as well as Thom Wolke's nature photography throughout these pages making The Green Songbook something new and unique. Thank you to the whole team at Alfred for going to great lengths to create this comprehensive project.

Truly, Guitars in the Classroom would not be here to make The Green Songbook without the team at NAMM, the International Music Products Association, GAMA, the Guitars and Accessories Marketing Association, John and Joan D'Addario and the D'Addario Music Foundation, the Music for Life Alliance, The Fender Music Foundation, and to Works of Life! It takes far more than a village to raise a program. To our faithful sponsors at The Martin Guitar Co., Godin Guitars, Greg Bennett and Samick Guitars, KAMAN Music Corp, D'Addario Strings, Levy's Leathers, Dunlop Manufacturing, Hohner USA, Daisy Rock Guitars, U.S. Music Corp, and Luna Guitars, thank you for keeping the music making free for America's teachers. We are all so blessed by your love and dedication to service, your concern for education and music making, and your extreme generosity. You make it happen.

Finally, I must include a note of personal thanks to Pete and Toshi Seeger for their inspirational advocacy for this beautiful blue planet. Their lifetimes of song, personal commitment and leadership, vibrant social action, and dedication to childrens' growing musicality have been a source of learning and inspiration throughout my life. May we carry on their message of hope for our planet with this publication.

Peace,

Jessica

Foreword

by Jessica Anne Baron
Founder & Executive Director, Guitars in the Classroom

This book and recording have been made by many hands, hearts and voices in an expression of love, wonder, gratitude, and concern that all our contributors—songwriters, artists, engineers, book makers, educators, photographers, and authors—feel for our home planet. Ten thousand words could hardly describe the profound importance of sustaining and nurturing this earth. We hope the 42 songs in this collection will serve as a worthy and compelling start.

Each song has been selected and all of them organized by chapters to focus on different aspects of eco-sustainability. Whether you are looking for just the right song to sing around a campfire, teach a science lesson, celebrate nature, lead a social change discussion, or inspire good habits with children, you will find songs to love and share in this book. We hope it becomes a treasure in your home and in the classrooms in your life; and that twenty years from now, when the planet is a healthier place, you will still have it sitting around, dog eared and loved.

This book comes at a time when we need to learn about our relationship to the planet, and to all creatures who share the land, water and sky. Lately, we have been experiencing many dramatic earth changes and challenges. Some have been natural occurrences for which human beings have been unprepared and unprotected- hurricanes and earthquakes have collapsed our structures, prevented access to clean water and electricity, and as a result, have caused illness and loss of life. At the same time, we have been experiencing human-made problems like mine explosions and oil spills that could and should have been prevented—if only people had been more careful, more mindful of the dangers involved in taking resources out of Mother Earth. These events are sad for us all, and we must learn from them to prevent more suffering in the future.

What does our earth need and how we can give these things to her? What must we change about our lives to live in harmony with her? *The Green Songbook* is meant to inspire us to ask and answer these questions and take important first steps in a positive direction. Not only will you find wise, powerful, and beautiful songs inside. You'll find advice and suggestions from leaders who have spent years growing their knowledge in order to pass it along to you. You'll find websites to visit, books to read, organizations to check out, and lists of things you can do at home and at school that will make your life and our planet "greener."

Truth be told, we can all learn to live more thoughtfully, more gracefully, and more responsibly on this planet. Every one of us is personally capable of making small changes that add up to reduce our carbon footprints and increase our benefit to all beings. We can use fewer precious resources, and have fun learning to use the ones we need more creatively and sparingly! We can preserve natural habitats and assist animals living there. We can participate in growing nourishing, natural food through practices that restore the balance of nature. Remembering to bring a canvas bag to the grocery store, to turn out the lights before we leave, to walk or ride a bike instead of automatically driving a car just because we can… these changes are easy to make if taken one at a time, day after day. We just need to know what to do, how to do it, and why it's important.

The Green Songbook will get you started and then some. It will present vision, hope, knowledge and encouragement, song after song, to make a vital difference in the way you walk through this world. In the words of songwriter David Pomerantz, "It's in every one of us to be wise." What a fun way to share our collective wisdom! So let us breathe deeply and take up musical instruments to sing these verses of praise, protection and promise for our planet, these choruses that confirm our commitment to every living thing.

About Guitars in the Classroom, an Educational Non-Profit Organization

This book has been created by Guitars in the Classroom, a California-based and nationally active non-profit organization that inspires, trains and equips general classroom teachers, specialists, and parent volunteers to integrate music and music making across the academic curriculum. GITC's board of directors developed the concept for this work, and GITC's founder and executive director, Jessica Anne Baron, has authored the book in collaboration with many dedicated and talented people. Pages 120–123 will introduce you to them.

Since 1998, Guitars in the Classroom (GITC) has been making daily music making in classrooms possible for students of all ages so that someday, every teacher and child can have access to making music and can become happier, more creative, and more successful at school.

GITC programs include "easy" group guitar instruction, singing and song-leading training, and collaborative songwriting coaching. Classes happen weekly on an ongoing basis through six sequential course levels, in accordance with educational content standards for music and academic subjects. Thanks entirely to the generosity of GITC's sponsors in the music products industry, teachers have always had free access to instruments, musical accessories, resource materials, and pedagogical support.

Guitars in the Classroom knows and trusts that music has the power to heal and strengthen our lives, schools, communities, and our planet. Through uniting teachers, school staff, and administrators with songwriters, performing artists, and music industry professionals, and with families, foundations, civic organizations, and philanthropically-minded individuals, we see how making music together does even more than helping children succeed as students. It revives and restores music to its rightful place in our schools and culture. We are entirely committed to this cause and hope you will join us. Together, we can make a difference.

For more information about Guitars in the Classroom's program and sponsors, please visit guitarsintheclassroom.org and stay updated on Facebook and Twitter.

The Songs

Songs can be poems or stories, prayers, revelations, hymns, protests, personal confessions and visions for humanity. Songs carry our traditions and shape our futures by crystallizing our thoughts and feelings, embedding them in rhythm, melody, and repetition. Songs come to visit and we invite the best ones to settle inside us for life. They become as essential as air, water, food, sunlight, as friendly as love, and as welcome as sleep. They live forever in our hearts, providing comfort, inspiration, humor, and memories. Life may be rough at times and unpredictable, but the songs we cherish never fail us.

The songs in this book have been selected for their beauty and the content of their lyrics, but also because they are relatively simple to sing and not too hard for a beginning guitarist to play. These songs also teach. They give us ideas to ponder, perspectives to try on, and suggestions for making our earth a healthier place. They remind us what we can do to have a positive influence on the planet. That's good because our lives are busy and we sometimes need reminding.

Everyone who helped make this book, from the songwriters to the artists, to the engineers in the recording studio want you and those in your circle of friends, family, and learning to have fun playing, singing, and sharing these songs. We hope many of them become your friends for life.

The Guitar Arrangements

Choose Your Chords

You will find that all the songs in this book are arranged in the key of "G." This helps beginners play the song with only a few simple chords. However, you can choose to play these songs in ANY key. To change the key, (or choose a key and chords not in "G"), please see p. 124 for a chart with other keys and their corresponding chords. Many of the songs in this book are arranged with basic chords so your fingers can successfully get from one to another without too much trouble. In some cases we have reduced the number of possible chord changes in a song so you'll have more time to focus on singing and you'll spend a bit less time than usual searching for the right places to put your fingers! We want you to ENJOY singing and playing these songs. Fewer chord changes lets you get in the strumming groove of a song and stay there! Please feel free to add complexity to any arrangement.

You will also notice some unusual chord charts at the top of each song. We have given you two sets of chords to choose from: GITC Chords and Standard Tuning Chords. Those of you who use the standard tuning chords will find those self-explanatory. Those of you who want to try something a little different, or easier than standard tuning chord shapes can try the "GITC Chords." GITC Chords show simplified fingerings, in Open G Tuning, as used by beginners in the GITC system. For many beginners, this approach is easier on the fingers and sounds really musical because the physical tasks involved in achieving tone and making chord changes are very achievable. Playing in Open G with easy chords means getting in a groove and singing without stopping between chord changes. The method lets you feel the flow of a song, even from the beginning.

Open G involves tuning three of your six strings (low E, A, and high E) down to D, G, and D respectively. This accomplishes three things:

1. Strumming the open (unfingered) strings will produce a lovely G chord. (Look Ma, no hands!)

2. Your guitar will be tuned lower which makes for a relaxed sound and feeling. Less tension on the strings, less tension in the music.

3. You can play simple chord changes with just one or two fingertips. Yes, some people like to cover many strings, even play some barre chords in Open G. Some like to play slide guitar in this tuning. Both work well.

The GITC method presents "easy" versions of chords that just take one new finger at a time *instead* of trying to place three fingers in awkward positions that require stretching and pressing down hard. By adding just one new skill at a time, as you are ready, learning to play guitar becomes a fun and painless experience. Eventually, you can learn all the other chords in standard tuning and it won't hurt. We transition from open tuning to standard tuning in our free GITC classes after 12 to 18 weeks depending on readiness.

Choosing and Changing Keys with a Capo

GITC teaches everyone how to use a capo to change the key in which you are playing so you can sing in the right key for your own voice and for children's voices. You will see a suggested capo position for each song.

If you capo your guitar in the suggested position, you can play right along with the CD recording that has come with this book! Please use the CD for your own practice and share it with children in your lives. We've selected keys for these songs that children will find are comfortable for their voices. Not too high or low. Just right. Of course you can also experiment with higher or lower capo positions to suit your own singing range, or the voices of your students. Music stores carry many kinds of capos and are happy to show the customer how each one works.

Choosing Different Strums

These arrangements also provide some suggestions for strumming patterns. We usually suggest the easiest one and something a little more elaborate as well.

Strumming patterns are a combination of two elements: the duration of the strum and its direction in a pattern. We can strum up and down in any combination. We can strum for a short time or a longer time, and we can combine long and short strums in any pattern we like. Strumming can be that simple!

The strum charts in these arrangements show you both elements together. For example, if you are strumming down to a slow, steady beat, the pattern looks like this:

If you are strumming down, then up, to the same beat, it looks this way:

You can hear these strumming patterns if you listen to the songs on the CD.

We were able to include many songs from this book on the recording, but not all. We'd like to suggest that you learn the strumming patterns using songs we did record, and then you will know how to play them for songs we did not record.

The songs we did not record are well known enough that you will be able to find them in a video format online. Then you can hear and SEE them being played! This of course is very fun to do and we recommend it, even if you like our recorded versions of the songs. There are so many ways to play and arrange any song, so it's great to compare and choose which arrangement you like most. Ours are simply designed to be sing-able, easy to play, and pretty.

Integrating a Song into a Lesson

Every song has a rhythm. Many have rhymes. All create feelings and images. These musical, literary, and sentient features embed content learning in an auditory and participatory package that grabs kids' attention and embed themselves in their memories. Songs are great big mnemonic devices that store far more valuable content than a phrase or an equation. So when you launch, deepen, or extend a lesson with a song, you are doing something almost magical to improve learning. Your students will thank you for this!

Most songs have words that can be removed and other words substituted and this is called "copy change songwriting." You can take almost any song and adapt it to teach what you have in your plans. This is the work of GITC. We can help you find the songs that are easiest to adapt. Many songs in this book lend themselves to students creating their own lyrics to enrich a lesson. Perhaps the best example is "Dolphins, Dolphins in the Sea" based on the universally beloved melody of "Twinkle, Twinkle Little Star."

Steve's suggestions below present some ideas that may seem very specific to his poem, "Habitat," but as a teacher, you already understand how to generalize a concept and apply it to something else. You do it every day! So, whether you love "Habitat" and share it with his lesson or not, everything he describes on the next page can be reworked to fit any song in this book!

We hope you'll take a minute to read Steve's lesson recommendations as a jumpstart to get you designing your own song-based lesson plans. He has given you a great start. It's true that when you add hand movements (think Total Physical Response or *TPR*) or large motor movements, some of your students' will devote more attention to learning and will learn better. If you extend the lesson with an art activity, collaborative or independent, you add deeper student connection to the lesson content through engaging the imagination and eliciting creative grapho-motoric skills and visual self expression. For visual-spatial learners and kinesthetic learners, this can be of tremendous benefit! If you tie the lesson to literature and independent reading, you also deepen content by associating ideas with characters and adventures,. This is a big plus for children who enjoy reading to themselves. Read that literature aloud and you'll have increased the value of the lesson for auditory learners, too. Really, you can't lose if you use a song! Additionally, kids will think you are the coolest teacher they know.

Please enjoy Steve Van Zandt's poem. You can visit him and his band, The Banana Slug String Band, online at www.bananaslugstringband.com for a free download of the poem as a song! The "Slugs" perform three songs from this book and Steve wrote them all. These include "The River Song," "Safe at Home," and the irresistible sing-along, "Dirt Made My Lunch."

HABITAT HABITAT
Steve Van Zandt

At the river side, the crayfish hide
While the fish jump high to catch a mayfly, in that *(chant softly) habitat, habitat*
In the pond what can be found, the reeds grow all around
Swimming pollywogs turn into jumping frogs, in that *habitat, habitat*
Now underneath the ground, the roots go pushing down
And the mole lives too, it finds an earthworm to chew in that *habitat, habitat*
Lift a log up nice and slow, a beetle crawls below
In decay that's where it feeds, watch out for centipede in that *habitat, habitat*

Chorus: Habitat, habitat, habitat there *(pause and point)*
Habitat, habitat is everywhere
That's the reason life can live
Food water shelter is what it gives
From the little micro clime to the big biome
Habitat, habitat, *Habitat's a home
With room to roam *Habitat's a home, *Habitat's a home

On a woodland trail, there are bushy grey tails
Into the trees they run away, as bobcat stalks its prey in that *habitat, habitat*
Out of the cave in the night, a million bats are taking flight
When morning sun comes around, they are sleeping upside down in that *habitat, habitat*
The prairie ripples in the breeze, field mice they are eating seeds
The snake slides by, away from hawk's sharp eye in that *habitat, habitat*
Habitat is what we need, so let's do a good deed
Keep it wild and free, protect diversity in that *habitat, habitat*

Chorus...

Coda: Prairie pond and underground
Log, cave, woodland, river
To habitat all life is bound
And that's why life can live here

Habitat: A Lesson Plan

1. Choral reading/put on overhead or smart board/break into groups alternating couplets and the "habitat, habitat" response. The last two lines of the chorus can be broken into two groups doing call and response; group one says; "habitat, habitat" group two yells "habitats a home" group one continues; "with room to room," group two completes the line with "habitats a home," then this last line is repeated. Repeat the coda several times. Try to memorize it.

2. Each couplet is a different habitat. Assign groups or individuals to illustrate their couplets. Assemble them as a book.

3. Use the lines as writing frames to write couplets for other habitats. Students write their own verses. Point out the AABB pattern in the rhyme. Brainstorm descriptors for other habitats. Point out that the lines in the song always contain an action and it shows the relationship between plants and animals.

4. Hold a debate with posters and even speaking about plants and animals for each habitat to argue why their particular habitat should not be turned into a parking lot.

5. Brainstorm a list of plants and animals that are unique to each habitat. Write each one on a separate card that is placed on each student's back. By asking yes and no questions to determine what is on their backs, students try to group themselves by habitat.

6. Students design a travel brochure and/or commercial for their habitat.

7. Use clay or multimedia to make sculptures of symbolic representations of the habitats.

8. Make up hand motions for the habitats that can be gestured while chanting the Coda. Use these same hand motions in a game where the leader, with his or her back to the group, says "One, two, three, what habitat will I be?" Right when the leader says "be," he/she turns around and assumes one of the habitat hand motions. Each person in the group displays a hand motion when the leader is saying one two three. Whoever has the same habitat as the leader is out until the next game. You might begin by agreeing on only three habitats.

9. Have students place sticks, boards, logs, bricks, etc. in places around the school yard and check underneath them every few days to see who has moved in.

10. Have students observe a tree to see who has made it their habitat. Return for follow-up observations.

Chapter 1
We Are the Change

A note to young readers from Jessica Anne Baron

In his historic speech of 1961, President John F. Kennedy inspired Americans to work together for peace saying, "Ask not what your country can do for you—ask what you can do for your country." Then, reaching out beyond American borders he continued, "My fellow citizens of the world: ask not what America will do for you, but what together we can do for the freedom of man."

President Kennedy challenged us to go beyond counting our blessings…to do something real and meaningful to give back and help others. Even greater still, he asked us to support and defend the idea of human freedom. This remarkable man's words inspired millions of people to work together for peace and justice around the world. And yet, he was just one person-with very human problems of his own. What if he had doubted his ability to move people to action? This nation and this world would be very different.

Let's follow his example and ask not what our beautiful and bountiful earth can do for us, but what we can do for the earth—and for every living creature! We know we are blessed to live on a planet that affords us food, shelter, warmth, heat, water, breathtaking beauty, the company of animals, and endless ways to have fun in nature. How will we show our gratitude and appreciation for these gifts? How will we nurture nature? What must we learn in order to make positive choices?

This book shares the knowledge and wisdom of many talented people who think about this all the time. They have come together with Guitars in the Classroom so you can learn ways to give back to our home planet and her inhabitants! You don't have to know much to begin. Simply sing a song and the answers will come. When you sing, others will listen and many will join you. They will learn, too. This is how you can help right now. You can make the music we all need to hear, you can inspire others to sing along, and because you choose to care and to sing, the planet will heal more and more. Remember President Kennedy's conviction and courage.

Like him, another visionary who changed our world, the beloved Mohandas "Mahatma" Ghandi, said it so simply: "Be the change you want to see in the world."

No need to wonder if your voice is strong enough. It surely is. Imagine one or two people in your life who you know will listen if you sing…and be brave. If you want a little extra musical support, sing along with the CD in this book. Trust that you are doing something really marvelous. You are shining your light. No matter what anyone thinks of that, you will know that you have expressed yourself. This is your birthright. In the words of the beloved spiritual leader Mohandas "Mahatma" Ghandi, "Be the change you want to see in the world."

WITH MY OWN TWO HANDS

Capo 5th Fret
Starting Pitch: 2nd fret, 4th string

Words and Music by
BEN HARPER

Standard Chords:

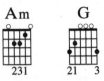

GITC Chords:

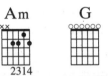

Strum:

Verse 1:

Am
Now I can change the world
       G   Am
With my own two hands.

Make it a better place
       G   Am
With my own two hands.

Make it a kinder place
       G   Am
With my own two hands.
       G   F   Am
With my own, with my own two hands.

Verse 2:

Am
Now I could make peace on earth
       G   Am
With my own two hands.

And I could clean up the earth
       G   Am
With my own two hands.

And I can reach out to you
       G   Am
With my own two hands.
       G   F   Am
With my own, with my own two hands.

Chorus:

G   Am
I'm gonna make it a   brighter place

          G
With my own...

                        Am
I'm gonna make it a   safer place

          G
With my own...

                  Am
I'm gonna help the   human race
          G   F   Am
With my own, with my own two hands.
          G   F   Am
With my own, with my own two   hands.

Verse 3:

Am   G   Am
Now I could hold you   with my own two hands.

                       G   Am
And I can comfort you   with my own two hands.

           G   F   Am
But you got to use,   use your own two hands.

F   G   F   Am
Use your own, use your own two hands.
          G   F   Am
I'm gonna use, use my own two hands.
          G   F   Am
With my own, with my own two hands.
          G   F   Am
With my own, with my own two hands.

IT'S IN EVERY ONE OF US

Capo 2nd Fret
Starting Pitch: Open, 3rd string

Words and Music by
DAVID POMERANZ

Standard Chords:

GITC Chords: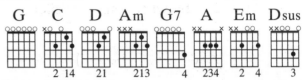

*The chords in this song go beyond the basic GITC chord fingerings.
Either use the standard tuning chords for this song,
or feel free to use the suggested, more advanced Open G tuning chords.

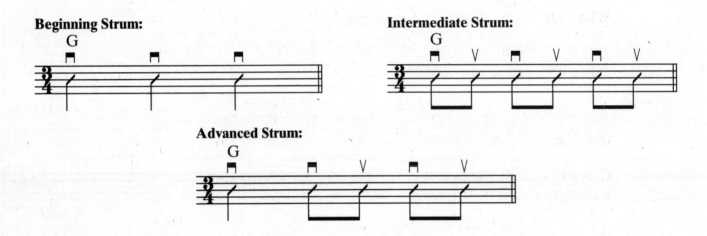

Beginning Strum:

Intermediate Strum:

Advanced Strum:

Chorus:

```
G           C  G              C  G    D
It's   in  every one  of  us  to  be  wise
Am  G   D              G   C  G
Find your heart, open up  both your eyes.
        C  D   Em              C           Dsus
We  can all know everything without ever knowing why
        G  C  G           C  G   D   C
It's   in  every one  of  us,  you  and  I.
```

Verse:

```
        G                   C   G
It's   in  every one  of  us, I  just remembered

        C           G      A
It's  like  I've  been sleeping for  years

        C
I'm  not  awake  as  I  can  be,

                      G
But  my   seeing  is  better

        Em                   A
I   can  see  through  the  tears
```

```
              G
I've    been    realizing that

      C              G
I   bought  this   ticket

                   C         G          A
And  I've  been  watching only  half  of  the  show
                   C                              G
And  there's  scenery  and  lights and  a    cast  of    thousands

              Em              A
Who   all   know  what  I    know

              Em            Dsus
And  it's   good that  it's   so...
```

Chorus:
```
              G C    G            C   G   D
It's    in    every  one  of  us  to  be  wise

C   G   D              G    C   G
Find your heart, open  up   both your  eyes.
         C   D    Em  G           C            Dsus
We  can all  know everything   without ever knowing why

              G C   G         C   G   D   Bm   C
It's    in    every one  of   us,  by  and  by.

              G C   G         C   G   D   C   G
It's    in    every one  of   us,  you and  I.
```

//Of all my songs, "It's in Every One of Us" is probably the most near and dear to my heart. The chorus expresses what I consider to be an ultimate truth—that we ALL instinctively know what is right and wrong, good and bad, constructive and destructive and have the power of choice to decide at every turn. It's a song about responsibility and the basic urge in every individual to do the right thing. Underneath it all, and in spite of much evidence to the contrary, I observe man to be basically "good" and not basically "bad" as some would have us believe. The song celebrates this fact and I trust that when push comes to shove, Man will come through and make this planet a garden once again. It is my privilege to have "It's in Every One of Us" be included in this book.//

–David Pomeranz

Chapter 2
A Loveable Planet

Image Credit: NASA

A note for teachers, parents, and friends
by Andrew Revkin

It's hard not to cherish life on Earth when you see a rainbow form, as sunlight penetrates sheets of rain beneath a departing thundercloud. Or when you regard the crystalline uniqueness of each snowflake alighting on a dark glove, or hear a coyote howl or loon call, or marvel at the flow of humanity in a great and thriving city. Good planets are indeed hard to find, as Steve Forbert sings and Carl Sagan, the astronomer and author, wrote so beautifully in his 1994 "Pale Blue Dot" speech and subsequent book. "Our planet is a lonely speck in the great enveloping cosmic dark," Sagan said, referring to a photograph taken of Earth in 1990 by the Voyager 1 spacecraft as it left the inner Solar System. The home planet is barely a pixel. "To me," he wrote, "it underscores our responsibility to deal more kindly with one another, and to preserve and cherish the pale blue dot, the only home we've ever known."

Any effort to preserve the ability of this planet to sustain humanity and the ecosystems around us has to start with some level of recognition of both the special nature of this orb *and* the unique responsibility that comes with humanness. As I've written before, while we have clearly become a planet-scale force, shaping ecosystems and the climate, we're hardly the first life form to do so. Cyanobacteria also were a planet-scale force, filling the atmosphere with the oxygen we now depend on. The difference is that cyanobacteria weren't *aware* of their potency, while we are at least starting to absorb that reality. I see this point in our history as a great, if uncomfortable, one—the moment when we embrace our place and new role, somewhat the way an adolescent takes on the tasks of adulthood.

How We Can Make a Difference

1. Get wet, cold, hot, high, low. Turn over a rock (carefully) to find the universe below.

2. Talk to a scientist about the Earth around you. They're not hard to find, and they don't bite.

3. Check out the small living places that Henry David Thoreau called "the swamp on the edge of town." National parks are great, but life is all around.

4. Use a telescope or microscope to put yourself in broader perspective.

5. Read some of the books listed below and share them with friends.

6. Find time in each day to step back a moment from the flow of toothbrushing and eating and work and studies to stop, take a breath, and marvel at the water, atmosphere, living things—and technologies—that make your life so remarkable.

Knowledge is Power: Where to Learn More

Places to Go

- Your front or back yard, but on your hands and knees.

- Your local natural history museum is a place where you might be able to meet and talk to a scientist, not to mention learn about the geology and biology that shapes the world around you.

- When you fly, try to take a few minutes away from the iPod or in-flight movie to stare out the window at the shapes of the clouds and the shifting landscapes below—ranging from farmland to forests to mountains to cities. It's a great way to recall the special nature of Earth.

- Water is such a profoundly important part of this living planet that it's worth reminding yourself where your water comes from. If you live in a town or city, visit its reservoir. If you live in the country, learn more about how wells work.

Books

- *Pale Blue Dot*, by Carl Sagan
- *Biophilia*, by E.O. Wilson
- *A Sand County Almanac*, by Aldo Leopold
- *Celebrations of Life*, by Rene Dubos
- *The Dream of the Earth*, by Thomas Berry
- *Last Child in the Woods*, by Richard Louv

Films

- *Koyaanisqatsi* - Life out of Balance
- *Earth—The Biography*, National Geographic
- *Planet Earth*, BBC, Discovery Channel
- *Wall-E*, Disney

Organizations

- The Aldo Leopold Foundation; aldoleopold.org
- The Thomas Berry Foundation; thomasberry.org
- The Children and Nature Network; childrenandnature.org
- The National Geographic Society; nationalgeographic.com
- The Sustainable Ecosystems Institute; sei.org

Websites

- The Planetary Society; http://www.planetary.org/explore/topics/voyager/pale_blue_dot.html
- NASA Earth Observatory; http://earthobservatory.nasa.gov
- Earth as Art Gallery; http://earthasart.gsfc.nasa.gov
- Dot Earth; http://nytimes.com/dotearth

Find these and many more helpful website addresses at www.greensongbook.com.

THIS PRETTY PLANET

Capo 7th Fret
Starting Pitch: Open 4th string

Words and Music by
TOM CHAPIN

Standard Chords:

GITC Chords:

Beginning Strum:

Intermediate Strum:

Advanced Strum:

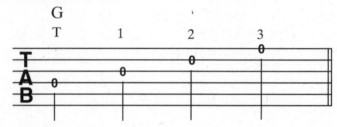

Part 1 Round:

G   Am
This pretty planet spinning through space,

            D   C   G
You're a garden, you're a harbor, you're a holy place.

Part 2 Round:

G   Am   D
Golden sun going down,   gentle blue giant,

C   G   Am   D   C   G
Spin us around   all through the night,   safe 'til the morning light.

GOOD PLANETS ARE HARD TO FIND

Capo 4th Fret
Starting Pitch: 3rd fret, 3rd string

Words and Music by
STEVE FORBERT

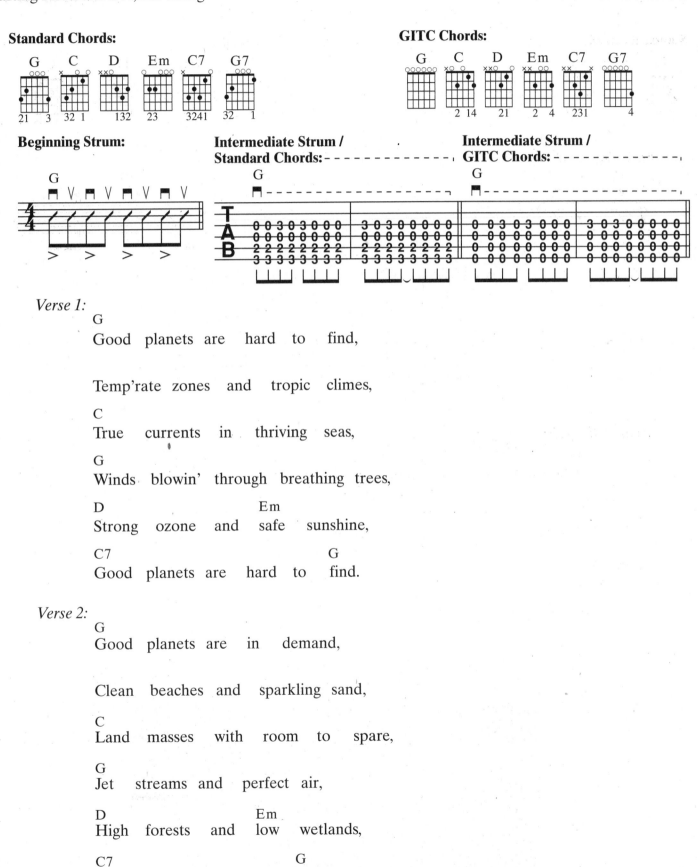

Verse 1:

G
Good planets are hard to find,

Temp'rate zones and tropic climes,

C
True currents in thriving seas,

G
Winds blowin' through breathing trees,

D   Em
Strong ozone and safe sunshine,

C7   G
Good planets are hard to find.

Verse 2:

G
Good planets are in demand,

Clean beaches and sparkling sand,

C
Land masses with room to spare,

G
Jet streams and perfect air,

D   Em
High forests and low wetlands,

C7   G
Good planets are in demand.

Chorus:

```
G7                          C7                          G7
And  the  mind  don't  know  if  the  heart  can't  see;

                            C7                D
Let  the  blind  man  go  to  his  destiny...
```

Verse 3:

```
G
Good  planets  are  rare  indeed,


Rain  fallin'  on  crops  and  seed,

C
Big  rivers  and  good  topsoil,

G
Fuel  sources  from  cane  to  oil,

D                        Em
Green  gardens  of  all  we  need,

C7                          G
Good  planets  are  rare  indeed.
```

Repeat Chorus:

Verse 4:

```
G
Good  planets  are  scarce  and  few,


Earthworms  and  caribou,

C
Strong  food  chains  and  tasty  meals,

G
Textiles  and  plants  that  heal,

D                        Em
Iron  mountains  and  skies  of  blue,

C7                              G
Good  planets  are  scarce  and  few.
```

Repeat Verse 1:

MOUNTAIN SONG

Capo 3rd Fret
Starting Pitch: 2nd fret, 4th string

Words and Music by
HOLLY NEAR

Standard Chords:

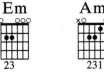

GITC Chords:

Strum:

Chorus 1:

Em
I have dreamed on this mountain

            Am   Em
Since first I was my mother's daughter.

            Em   C   Em
And you can't just take my dreams away – not with me watching.

You may drive a big machine

            Am   Em
But I was born a great big woman.

            Em   C   Em
And you can't just take my dreams away – not with me fighting.

Verse:

Em
This old mountain raised my many daughters

Am
Some died young – some are still living.

                        Em
But if you come here for to take our mountain,

           Am   Em
Well, we ain't come here to give it.

Chorus 2:

Em
I   have   dreamed   on   this   mountain

            Am   Em
Since   first   I   was   my   mother's   daughter.

            Em   C   Em
And you can't just take my dreams away – not with me watching.

            Em   C   Em
No, you can't just take my dreams away – without me fighting.

            Em   C   Em
No, you can't just take my dreams away.

Repeat Chorus 1, Verse, & Chorus 2:

COUNTRY ROADS

Capo 5th Fret
Starting Pitch: Open 4th string

Words and Music by
JOHN DENVER

Standard Chords:

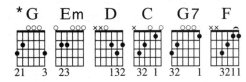

GITC Chords:

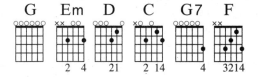

*The chords in this song go beyond the basic GITC chord fingerings.
Either use the standard tuning chords for this song,
or feel free to use the suggested, more advanced Open G tuning chords.

Beginning Strum:

Intermediate Strum:

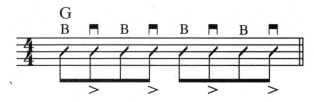

Verse 1:

G   Em
Almost heaven, West Virginia

D   C   G
Blue Ridge mountains, Shenandoah River.

G   Em
Life is old there, older than the trees,,

D   C   G
Younger than the mountains, growing like a breeze.

Chorus:

G   D
Country roads, take me home,

               Em   C
To the place where I belong,

              G   D
West Virginia, mountain mama.

                 C   G
Take me home, country roads.

Verse 2:

G   Em
All   my   mem'ries gather 'round her,

D   C   G
Miner's lady, stranger to blue waters.

G   Em
Dark and dusty painted on the sky,

D   C   G
Misty taste of moonshine, teardrop in my eye.

Repeat Chorus:

Bridge:

Em   D   G   G7
I   hear her voice, in the mornin' hours she calls me

           C   G   D
The radio reminds me of my home far away.

Em   F   C
Driving down the road I get a   feeling

           G   D
That I should have been home yesterday, yesterday.

Repeat Chorus 2 times:

THE EARTH IS OUR MOTHER

Capo 7th Fret
Starting Pitch: 2nd fret, 4th string

Traditional

Standard Chords:

Em   C

23   32 1

GITC Chords:

Em   C

2 4   2 14

Strum:

Em

$\frac{4}{4}$

Verse 1:

Em   C
The   earth   is   our   mother.   We   must   take   care   of   her.

Em   C   Em
The   earth   is   our   mother.   We   must   take   care   of   her.

Refrain:

Em   C   Em   C
Hey   yanna   ho   yanna   hey   yan   yan,   hey   yanna   ho   yanna   hey   yan   yan.

Verse 2:

Em   C
The   sacred   ground   we   walk   upon   with   every   step   we   take.

Em   C   Em
The   sacred   ground   we   walk   upon   with   every   step   we   take.

Refrain:

Em   C   Em   C
Hey   yanna   ho   yanna   hey   yan   yan,   hey   yanna   ho   yanna   hey   yan   yan.

Verse 3:

Em   C
The   sky   is   our   father.   We   must   take   care   of   him.

Em   C   Em
The   sky   is   our   father.   We   must   take   care   of   him.

Refrain:

Em   C   Em   C
Hey   yanna   ho   yanna   hey   yan   yan,   hey   yanna   ho   yanna   hey   yan   yan.

Em   C   Em
Hey   yanna   ho   yanna   hey   yan   yan,   hey   yanna   ho   yanna   hey   yan   yan.

THIS LAND IS YOUR LAND

Capo 7th Fret
Starting Pitch: Open 3rd string

Words and Music by
WOODY GUTHRIE

Standard Chords:

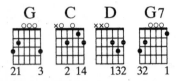

GITC Chords:

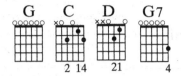

Beginning Strum:

Intermediate Strum:

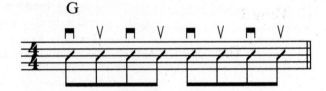

Advanced Strum

Chorus:

```
        G                  C                      G
        This land is    your land, this land is   my land

                         D                        G        G7
        From Cali - fornia to    the  New York  Island

                                 C                            G
        From  the   red - wood  forest,  to   the   gulfstream waters

        D                              G        G7
        This  land  was  made  for  you  and  me.
```

Verse 1:

```
                         C                        G
        As  I   was  walking  a   ribbon  of   highway

                              D                    G
        I    saw  a - bove  me   an   endless  skyway

                              C                    G
        I    saw  be - low  me   a    golden  valley

        D                              G        G7
        This  land  was  made  for  you  and  me.
```

Verse 2:

                 C   G

I've roamed and rambled and I've followed my footsteps

                  D   G

To the sparkling sands of her diamond deserts

              C   G

And all a - round me a voice was sounding

D   G   G7

This land was made for you and me.

Repeat Chorus:

Verse 3:

                  C   G

The sun comes shining as I was strolling

                  D   G

The wheat fields waving and the dust clouds rolling

                  C   G

The fog was lifting a   voice come chanting

D   G   G7

This land was made for you and me.

Repeat Chorus:

Verse 4:

                        C   G

As   I   was   walkin' I   saw   a   sign there

                D   G

And that sign said, "No tress - passin'"

                C   G

But on the other side it didn't say nothin!

       D   G   G7

Now that side was made for you and me!

Repeat Chorus:

Chapter 3
Life Giving Waters

by Mark Rauscher

My name is Mark Rauscher; I'm the Director of Beach Programs for the Surfrider Foundation. Surfrider is a non-profit grassroots environmental organization focused on coastal conservation. We accomplish this through the hard work of thousands of volunteers in over 70 community chapters around the U.S. and globally.

Growing up as a surfer in Florida, I always had a strong connection with the ocean and the beach, and I was fortunate to be able to study Oceanography in college, learning about the many threats to the health of our ocean and beaches.

When we think of water, we probably either think of the water we drink or the water we surf in. What we often miss is that these two types of water are connected. Water is a finite resource...there isn't any "new" water being created. All water on the planet has been recycled since day one on this planet, and our choices as surfers play a role in that cycle.

We know that the water we see going down street drains, picking up and transporting a toxic cocktail of pollutants ends up in the ocean. The reality is that we are not bystanders of that simple act of pollution—we're impacted by it directly. The water picks up pollution and then drains to the ocean. We surf in that ocean. We get sick. Many of us get shots to prevent us from getting sick. This is our reality.

Sure, we know about the water cycle (water from the ocean evaporates, forms clouds, rains, and becomes drinking water, etc.) but it is easy to forget how our daily choices are either part of the solution or the problem. We're affected by choices like how people get rid of dog poop or what they do with expired prescription drugs. If dog poop isn't picked up, then it's right there with us as we dive through a wave. If our friends flush prescription drugs down the toilet, those drugs eventually end up in our ocean. We're not just bystanders in this—we're surfers. We're in the water and water is in us. So as one surfer to another, the next time you see water, whether it's heading down the drain or coming from your faucet, take a moment to connect the dots. That next toilet flush may just be the water in your next barrel—hopefully it'll be a clean barrel.

How We Can Make a Difference

1. Pick up your pet's wastes. Pet waste that reaches the ocean can make both people and marine life sick!

2. Get the adults and teens around you to hold on to their butts! It's best not to smoke, but if people you know do, ask them to dispose of their used cigarettes in a proper waste container. Cigarette butts are the number one litter component found on the beach!

3. Don't hose down your driveways. Not only does it waste water, but it causes oils and other pollutants to end up in our oceans. Use a broom and dust pan instead.

4. Plant native or climate-adapted plants in your garden. These kinds of plants use less water, which helps reduce runoff and helps keep our beaches clean.

5. When you go to beach, make sure you not only pick up your trash, try and pick up at least one piece of somebody else's. If everyone did this, we'd have our beaches and coastlines looking better in no time!

6. Cut back on your family's use of fertilizers. Excess fertilizers that make it into our waterways can cause harmful plankton blooms that can harm fish, marine mammals and other sea life.

7. Avoid using single-use plastic bottles and bags. These and other types of plastics often end up on our beaches and in our oceans, where they harm birds, sea turtles and other marine life. Instead, use refillable bottles and reusable bags and containers.

8. Volunteer with a local environmental organization. Your time and effort goes a long way to improving the health of our neighborhoods and ecosystem.

Some Interesting Facts about Water

- Most people realize that hot water uses up energy, but supplying and treating cold water requires a significant amount of energy too. American public water supply and treatment facilities consume about 56 billion kilowatt-hours per year—enough electricity to power more than 5 million homes for an entire year.

- About 75 percent of the water we use in our homes is used in the bathroom.

- If your toilet is from 1992 or earlier, you probably have an inefficient model that uses between 3.5 to 7 gallons per flush. Newer, high-efficiency toilets use less than 1.3 gallons per flush—that's at least 60 percent less water per flush!

- The average bathroom faucet flows at a rate of two gallons per minute. Turning off the tap while brushing your teeth in the morning and at bedtime can save up to eight gallons of water per day, which equals 240 gallons a month.

- Letting your faucet run for five minutes uses about as much energy as letting a 60-watt light bulb run for 14 hours.

- Leaky faucets that drip at the rate of one drip per second can waste more than 3,000 gallons of water each year; A leaky toilet can waste about 200 gallons of water every day. If your fixtures have leaks, you should get them repaired!

- A full bath tub requires about 70 gallons of water, while taking a five-minute shower uses only 10 to 25 gallons.

- The typical single-family suburban household uses at least 30 percent of their water outdoors for irrigation. Some experts estimate that more than 50 percent of landscape water use goes to waste due to evaporation or runoff caused by over watering! Consider installing a drip irrigation system to water your lawn and garden!

These facts come from the Oberlin College Resource Conservation Team! You can read more at www.oberlin.edu/recycle/facts.

Knowledge is Power: Where to Learn More

Books

- *Water Dance*, by Thomas Locker
- *The Snowflake a Water Cycle Story*, by Neil Waldman
- *A Drop around the World*, by Barbara Shaw McKinney and Michael S. Maydak
- *Chicken Soup for the Ocean Lover's Soul*, by Jack Canfield, Mark Hansen and Wyland
- *50 Ways to Save the Ocean*, by David Helvarg
- *Surfer's Code: 12 Simple Lessons for Riding Through Life*, by Shaun Tomson

Documentaries

- *Blue Gold: World Water Wars*; www.bluegold-worldwaterwars.com
- *Flow*; www.flowthefilm.com
- *Water Voices* (documentary series); www.adb.org/Water/Knowledge-Center/dvds/water-voices.asp
- *The Cycle of Insanity*; www.knowyourh2o.org
- *From Sea to Summit: A Journey Through the Watershed*; www.surfrider.org/seatosummit.asp
- *Sharkwater*; www.sharkwater.com

Organizations

- Kokua Hawaii Foundation's Plastic Free Schools Program; www.kokuahawaiifoundation.org/plasticfreeschools
- The Surfrider Foundation; www.surfrider.org
- Charity: Water bringing safe drinking water to people in developing nations; www.charitywater.org
- Clearwater Environmental Organization; www.clearwater.org/festival/aboutclearwater.html
- Rise Above Plastics; www.riseaboveplastics.org
- WaterKeeper Alliance; www.waterkeeper.org
- Save the Waves; www.savethewaves.org
- Heal the Bay; www.healthebay.org

Websites

- The EPA's "Our Waters" page introduces all kinds of water systems; www.water.epa.gov/type
- The Real Story of Water; www.knowyourh2o.org
- A Coastal Knowledge Resource; www.beachapedia.org
- The Clean Water Act; www.wikipedia.org/wiki/Clean_Water_Act

Find these and many more helpful website addresses at www.greensongbook.com.

TALK OF THE TOWN

Capo 4th Fret
Starting Pitch: Open 2nd string

Words and Music by
JACK JOHNSON

Standard Chords:

*C   D   G   Am   Cm

32 1   132   21 3   231   13421 3fr.

*The chords in this song go beyond the basic GITC chord fingerings.
Either use the standard tuning chords for this song,
or feel free to use the suggested, more advanced Open G tuning chords.

GITC Chords:

C   D   G   Am   Cm

2 1   21   2314   2 3

Beginning Strum:

C

Intermediate Strum:

C

Verse 1:

C   Am
I want to be where the talk of the town

D   G
Is about last night when the sun went down.

C   Am   D
Yeah, and the trees all dance and the warm wind blows

G   C
In that same old sound.

Verse 2:

Am   D
And the water below gives a gift to the sky,

G   C
And the clouds give back every time they cry,

Am   D
And make the grass grow green beneath my toes.

G
And, if the sun comes out,

C
I'll paint a picture all about

Am
The colors I've been dreaming of.

D
The hours just don't seem enough

Am
To put it all together.

D   G
Maybe it's as strange as it seems

C   G   C
Mmmm mmmm...

32

Verse 3:

```
C          Am                      D
And the trouble I find is that the trouble finds me.
          G                   C
It's a part of my mind, it begins with a dream,
          Am                   D
And a feeling I get when I look and I see
          G                 C
That this world is a puzzle. Find all of the pieces
          Am                   D
And put it all together, and then I'll rearrange it,
          Am
And follow it    forever.
D                              G
Always be as strange as it seems
          C     G   C
Mmmm  mmmm...
```

Bridge:

```
  Cm                         Am   D G  C
Nobody ever told me not to try...

       Am D          G   C
Not to try,      oh, let's try.
          Am D          G   C
Yeah, let's try... oh, let's try.
```

Repeat Verse 2:

Bridge:

```
  Cm                       Am   D G C
Nobody ever told me not to try...

       Am D          G  C
Not to try,     oh, let's try.
          Am D         G  C G C G C G C G
Yeah, let's try... oh, let's try.
```

WATER CYCLE

Capo 5th Fret
Starting Pitch: 3rd fret, 1st string

Words and Music by
BONNIE LOCKHART

Standard Chords:

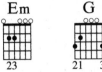
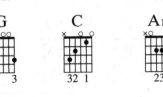

GITC Chords:

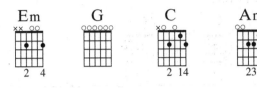

Beginning Strum:

Intermediate Strum:

Verse 1:

```
     G          Em              G
From the   clouds, to   the   snow,
              Em              G
To   the   mountains  down below.
              Em        G
Melting   rain,    waterfall,
              C                G
To   the   lake  that  holds  it   all.
```

Chorus:

```
          Em                    C              Am
It's  a   cycle,  it's  a  circle,  it's  a   dancer,  watch  her  spin.
          Em                    C            G
And  the   water  coming  to  us,  it  goes  'round  and  'round  again.
```

Verse 2:

```
          Em              G
Aqueduct  from    the   lake

               Em             G
Brings  the   water  that  we   take.

               Em       G
From  the   pipes  underground

               C               G
To   the   faucet  where  it's   found.
```

Repeat Chorus:

Verse 3:

           Em   G

Wash your hands, wash your clothes,

           Em   G

But remember where it goes.

           Em   G

To the ground from the drain,

           C   G

Back into the clouds again.

Repeat Chorus:

Verse 4:

           Em   G

Every leaf, every child,

           Em   G

Every creature in the wild,

         Em   G

Everyone, everywhere,

           C   G

Needs the water that we share.

Chorus:

           Em   C   Am

It's a cycle, it's a circle, it's a dancer, watch her spin.

           Em   C   G

And the water coming to us, it goes 'round and 'round again,

           C   G   C   G

It goes 'round and 'round again, it goes 'round and 'round again.

RIVER SONG

Capo 3rd Fret
Starting Pitch: Open, 4th string

Words and Music by
STEVE VAN ZANDT
with the BANANA SLUG STRING BAND

Standard Chords:

G   C   D

GITC Chords:

G   C   D

Beginning Strum:

Intermediate Strum:

Advanced Strum (Travis pick):

Verse 1:

```
G                    C        G            D
It happened one day on a mountain so high,
G          C        D            G
A river was born from out of the sky.
G          C      G         D
The rain and the snow came falling down,
        G          C        D       G
And they started to run as they hit the ground.
```

Chorus:

```
G          C       G        D
Blurp-ah-pa-shoosh rum-bl-ly   pound
    G          C          D        G
A white rapid river makes a wonderful sound.
G          C      G          D
Blurp-ah-pa-shoosh rum-bl-ly   pound
```

```
    G              C            D         G
A white rapid river makes a wonderful sound.
```

Verse 2:

```
G                  C         G          D
Over beds made of granite it swept and it rolled,
       G          C        D      G
It was narrow and steep and so icy cold.
G              C           G             D
It carved out a valley and gouged out the land,
       G          C       D           G
It carried small rocks and it ground them to sand.
```

Verse 3:

```
   G                    C              G              D
It  filled  up  a  lake  and  was  still  for  a  day,
   G                    C           D              G
But  soon  that  wide  river  went  along  on  its  way.
   G                    C           G              D
It  rolled  past  rocks  and  banks  lined  with  trees,
         G              C         D            G
It  carried  small  boats  of  fall  colored  leaves.
```

Repeat Chorus:

Verse 4:

```
   G                    C              G           D
It  wound  and  it  wound  till  it  wound  past  me,
         G              C              D        G
And  I  knew  it  was  happy,  it  was  wild  and  free.
   G                 C              G          D
I  knew  it  was  happy,  it  was  wild  and  free,
         G              C         D            G
But  I  waved  it  goodbye  as  it  entered  the  sea.
```

Verse 5:

```
   G                    C           G              D
The  water  in  the  sea  soon  rose  to  the  sky
            G              C         D              G
And  the  wind  blew  a  cloud  to  the  mountain  so  high.
   G                    C    G         D
The  rain  and  the  snow  came  falling  down
         G              C       D          G
And  flowed  to  the  river  as  they  hit  the  ground.
```

Chorus:

```
   G              C       G         D
Blurp - ah - pa - shoosh  rum - bl - ly  pound
      G              C            D           G
A  white  rapid  river  makes  a  wonderful  sound.
   G              C    G            D
Blurp - ah - pa - shoosh  rum - bl - ly  pound
      G              C            D           G
A  white  rapid  river  makes  a  wonderful  sound.
      G              C         D           G
A  white  rapid  river  makes  a  wonderful  sound.
```

THE WHEEL OF THE WATER

Capo 3rd Fret
Starting Pitch: Open 4th string

Words and Music by
TOM CHAPIN

Standard Chords:

GITC Chords:

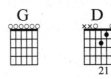

Strum:

Refrain:

           G
And the wheel of the water goes 'round and around,

                             D
And the wheel of the water goes 'round.

           G
And the wheel of the water goes 'round and around,

                             D
And the wheel of the water goes 'round.

Verse 1:

   G
Water flow down, down, trickle, trickle down.

                 D
Down to the ocean, trickle, trickle down.

   G
Water flow down, down, trickle, trickle down

                 D
Down to the ocean, trickle, trickle down.

Verse 2:

G
See the vapors rise,
                    D
See them cloud the skies.
G
See the vapors rise,
                    D
See them cloud the skies.

Verse 3:

G
Clouds rain down,
                    D
Thunder and lightning sound.

G
Clouds rain down,
                    D
Thunder and lightning sound.

Verse 4:

G
Springs bubble bubble up,
               D
Springs bubble up.
G
Springs bubble bubble up,
               D
Springs bubble up.

Refrain:

               G
And the wheel of the water goes 'round and around,
                                  D
And the wheel of the water goes 'round.

               G
And the wheel of the water goes 'round and around,
                                  D
And the wheel of the water goes 'round.

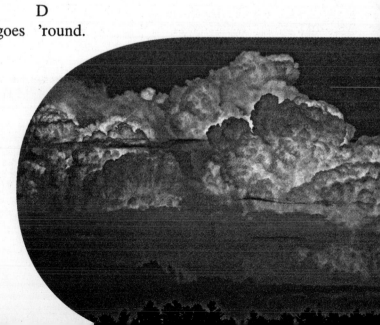

Chapter 4
Healthy Habitats

by Jessica Anne Baron

If you take a walk in your neighborhood, no matter where you live, you can discover your own habitat in action. Every living creature plays a part—from earthworms and mosquitoes to domestic pets and farm animals, wild animals such as raccoons and mice, and our own species—human beings (or homo sapiens). Whether you live in a big- or mid-sized city, in a suburb, in a small town, or out "in the country," away from cities and towns, your habitat is teaming with wildlife! The grass, flowers, plants and trees feed the soil, the bugs, and the animals; and they purify the air so we can breathe.

Imagine how many others depend on that very same habitat just as you do. Within your habitat, every creature—from bacteria and mold right on up to towering trees, from caterpillars to coyotes has a role to play to help the whole environment stay healthy. This web of interconnectedness supports us all. When the web is damaged and one of us is threatened, we are all affected. Tuning into this interconnectedness, learning how it works, and finding ways to live in balance with your fellow plants and animals will make it possible to preserve our natural habitats.

In one of many famous and moving quotations about the relationship between humans and nature, Chief Seattle wisely reminded us, "Humankind has not woven the web of life. We are but one thread within it. Whatever we do to the web, we do to ourselves. All things are bound together. All things connect." With this mindfulness, it gets easier to see how one good decision on your part can benefit everyone around you. When you pick up a single piece of trash and recycle it or throw it away, you are respecting and helping many living creatures. And if you do it, the chance that your friends will help out, too, goes way up. May you walk lightly in nature, notice her beauty and her delicate qualities, and give her the love and respect she needs to thrive.

How We Can Make a Difference

1. Get to know your habitat. List every living creature you know of that shares your environment within a mile. Take a walk and write down each one you see. Take pictures too! Then you can make a habitat collage, book, or PowerPoint presentation to share.

2. Learn what species in your habitat need help to survive. Which ones are threatened and by what? You can learn about this from the world wildlife fund, from the U.S. Fish and Wildlife Service, and by asking your science teacher for help.

3. Choose an animal you find interesting from your habitat and observe them over five mornings and twilights (feeding time for many animals) to see what they do, like, eat, and what threatens them. Birds make wonderful subjects for regular observation.

4. Learn about the water in your habitat. Where does it gather naturally? Is there a pond, lagoon, wetland, stream, river, lake, or ocean near you? How clean is that water? Does it contain harmful chemicals? Ask your local water provider to educate you about the local water supply; then visit your local water sanitation plant to learn about how your waste water is treated before it is returned to you through your own taps at home.

5. Nurture nature in your own small way. Grow a garden of your own in a window box, a pot, or in your yard. Know what plants will make the local birds and butterflies happy. For instance, cone flowers (Echinacea, *Echinacea purpurea*) are easy to grow and they attract monarch butterflies which feed black-headed grosbeaks and black-backed orioles.

6. Join a club to create a community garden at school, or in your neighborhood. Learn more about community gardening and its many benefits from The American Community Gardening Association's website (www.communitygarden.org)

Knowledge is Power: Where to Learn More

Books
- *Planet Patrol: A Kids' Action Guide to Earth Care*, by Maybeth Lorbiecki
- *Jungle Days Jungle Nights*, by Martin and Tanis Jordan
- *A Forest Habitat*, by Bobbie Kalman
- *Animal Habitats!* (Williamson Little Hands Series), by Judy Press and Betsy Day
- *Look Closer—Rainforest*, by Barbara Taylor
- *Rain Forest Secrets*, by Arthur Dorros
- *World of the Rain Forest*, by Rosie McCormick
- *I See a Kookaburra!: Discovering Animal Habitats Around the World*, by Jenkins and Page

Organizations
- The National Resources Defense Council; www.savebiogems.org
- The Izaak Walton League of America; www.iwla.org
- The National Audubon Society; www.conservation.audubon.org
- The Association of Zoos and Aquariums; www.aza.org
- The Wildlife Conservation Society; www.wcs.org/saving-wild-places.aspx
- The Sierra Club; www.sierraclub.org

Websites
- The Environmental Protection Agency's kids page; www.epa.gov/kids
- Defenders of Wildlife's Kids Page; www.kidsplanet.org
- US Fish and Wildlife Service, Endangered Species Program; www.fws.gov/endangered
- Audubon Society's Kids Page; www.audubon.org/educate/kids
- The Rainforest Alliance's Kids Page; www.rainforest-alliance.org/education.cfm?id=kidsmain
- The Ecology Fund helps all kinds of habitat preservation projects through online marketing; www.ecologyfund.com/ecology/_ecology.html
- The USDA's Backyard Conservation Guide; www.ldaf.state.la.us/portal/Portals/0/SWC/Conservation%20Education/backyardbookle.pdf

Find these and many more helpful website addresses at www.greensongbook.com.

HABITAT

Capo 5th Fret
Starting Pitch: Open 3rd string

Words and Music by
BILL OLIVER

Standard Chords:

GITC Chords:

Beginning Strum: shuffle

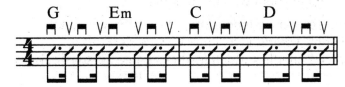

Advanced Strum: Travis-Country

Chorus:

G   Em   C   D
Habitat, habitat, have to have a habitat.

G   Em   C   D
Habitat, habitat, have to have a habitat.

G   Em   C   D
Habitat, habitat, have to have a habitat.

    D   G
You have to have a habitat to carry on!

Verse 1:

        G   Em   C   D
The ocean is a habitat, a very special habitat.

        G   Em
It's where the deepest water's at,

        C   D
It's where the biggest mammal's at.

        G   Em
It's where our future food is at,

        C   D
It keeps the atmosphere intact.

        D   G
The ocean is a habitat that we depend on!

42

Repeat Chorus:

Verse 2:

```
              G           Em        C           D
The   forest  is  a  habitat, a   very  special  habitat.

              G                 Em
It's   where  the  tallest  trees  are   at,

              C                      D
It's   where  a   bear  can  scratch her  back.


(ch - ch - ch - ch - ch - ch - ch)

              G                      Em
It   keeps  the  ground from  rolling back,

       C               D
Renews  the   oxygen, in    fact,

       D                                    G
The  forest  is  a  habitat that  we  depend on!
```

Repeat Chorus:

Verse 3:

```
              G           Em        C           D
The   river  is  a  habitat, a   very  special  habitat.

              G                  Em
It's   where  the  freshest  water's  at,

       C                D
For  people, fish,  and   muskrat.

G                    Em
But   when  people  dump  their  trash,

       C.              D
The   rivers  take  the  biggest rap.

       D                                G
The  river  is  a  habitat that  we  depend on!
```

Repeat Chorus:

Verse 4:

```
        G           Em          C           D
Now, people are  different than foxes  and  rabbits,

G               Em          C           D
Effect the  whole world with  our  bad  habits.

G           Em              C           D
Better to   love  it   while  we   still  have  it,

    D                               G
Or  rat – ta - tat - tat,  our  habitat's  gone!
```

Chorus:

```
G       Em      C                   D
Habitat, habitat, have  to   have  a   habitat.

G       Em      C                   D
Habitat, habitat, have  to   have  a   habitat.

G       Em      C                   D
Habitat, habitat, have  to   have  a   habitat.

    D                                   G
You  have  to   have  a   habitat to   carry  on!

    D                                   G
You  have  to   have  a   habitat to   carry  on!

    D                                   G
You  have  to   have  a   habitat to   carry  on!
```

SAFE AT HOME

Capo 5th Fret
Starting Pitch: Open 2nd string

Words and Music by
STEVE VAN ZANDT
with the BANANA SLUG STRING BAND

Standard Chords:

GITC Chords:

Beginning Strum:

Intermediate Strum:

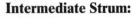
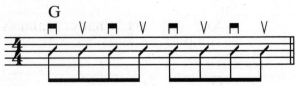

Advanced Strum (Travis Pick):

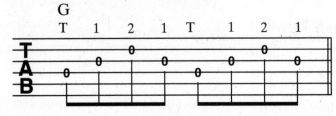

Verse 1:

G
One baby otter in the cradle of the sea,

C   G
Two baby owls in the hollow of a tree,

C   G
Three baby fawn in the forest where they've grown,

G   D   G
And all the baby animals are safe at home,

G   D   G
And all the baby animals are safe at home.

Verse 2:

G
Four baby bears coming home to rest,

C   G
Five baby mice are sleeping in their nest,

C   G
Six baby chicks to the coup they have gone,

G   D   G
And all the baby animals are safe at home,

G   D   G
And all the baby animals are safe at home.

Verse 3:

G
Seven baby pigs all snuggled in their pen,
C   G
Eight baby fox are lying in their den,
C   G
Nine baby geese back to the weeds have flown,

G   D   G
And all the baby animals are safe at home,
G   D   G
And all the baby animals are safe at home.

Verse 4:

G
One cradle rocking by the warm fire light,
C   G
One child sleeping peaceful in the night,
C   G
Love is the reason you'll never feel alone
G   D   G
Like all the baby animals safe at home,
G   D   G
All the baby animals safe at home,

G   D   G
All the baby animals safe at home.

PARADISE

Capo 3rd Fret
Starting Pitch: Open 3rd string

Words and Music by
JOHN PRINE

Standard Chords:

GITC Chords:

Beginning Strum:

Intermediate Strum:

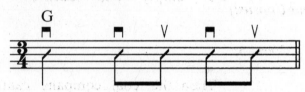

Verse 1:

G		Csus	G

When I was a child, my family would travel

	D	G

Down to Western Kentucky where my parents were born.

	Csus	G

And there's a backwards old town that's often remembered

	D	G

So many times that my memories are worn.

Chorus:

G		Csus	G

And daddy won't you take me back to Muhlenberg County,

	D	G

Down by the Green River where Paradise lay.

	Csus	G

Well, I'm sorry, my son, but you're too late in asking,

	D	G

Mister Peabody's coal train has hauled it away.

Verse 2:

```
    G                                    Csus            G
    Well,  sometimes   we'd  travel  right   down  the  Green  River
```

```
                                          D         G
    To    the    abandoned   old   prison   down    by   Adrie   Hill.
```

```
                                        Csus          G
    Where  the  air  smelled  like  snakes  and  we'd   shoot  with  our   pistols,
```

```
                              D            G
    But   empty   pop   bottles   was    all   we   would   kill.
```

Repeat Chorus:

Verse 3:

```
    G                                    Csus            G
    Then  the  coal  company  came  with  the   world's  largest   shovel,
```

```
                                        D            G
    And   they   tortured   the   timber   and   stripped   all   the   land.
```

```
                                          Csus      G
    Well,  they  dug  for  their  coal  till   the   land  was   forsaken,
```

```
                                        D            G
    Then   they   wrote   it   all   down   as   the   progress   of   man.
```

Repeat Chorus:

Verse 4:

```
    G                                    Csus            G
    When  I  die,  let  my  ashes  float   down  the  Green   River.
```

```
                                        D            G
    Let   my   soul   roll   on   up   to   the   Rochester   Dam.
```

```
                                          Csus      G
    I'll  be  halfway  to  Heaven  with   Paradise   waitin',
```

```
                                        D            G
    Just   five   miles   away   from   wherever   I   am.
```

Repeat Chorus:

BIG YELLOW TAXI

Capo 8th Fret
Starting Pitch: Open 3rd string

Words and Music by
JONI MITCHELL

Standard Chords:

GITC Chords:

Beginning Strum:

Intermediate/Advanced Strum:

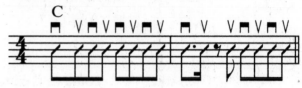

Verse 1:

G   C
They paved paradise,

                    G
Put up a parking lot.

         C   D
With a pink hotel, a boutique,

            G
And a swinging hot spot.

Chorus:

G
Don't it always seem to go

        C   G
That you don't know what you've got till it's gone.

        C   D   G
They paved paradise, put up a parking lot.

Verse 2:

        C
They took all the trees

                  G
Put 'em in a tree museum.

        C
And they charged the people

D   G
A dollar and a half just to see 'em.

Repeat Chorus:

Verse 3:

        C   G

Hey farmer, farmer, put away the DDT now.

                C

Give me spots on my apples,

        D   G

But leave me the birds and the bees, please!

Repeat Chorus:

Verse 4:

    C   G

Late last night I heard my screen door slam.

              C

And a big yellow taxi

    D   G

Took away my old man.*

Chorus:

    G

Don't it always seem to go

                C   G

That you don't know what you've got till it's gone.

              C   D   G

They paved paradise, put up a parking lot.

*Lyrics footnote: If you are singing this song with children, you may want to substitute the lyric "best friend" for "old man" since it describes children's experiences more accurately.

AIR

Capo 3rd Fret
Starting Pitch: Open 3rd string

Words and Music by
STUART STOTTS

Standard Chords:

GITC Chords:

Beginning Strum:

Intermediate Strum:

Advanced Strum:

Verse 1:

G
Once there was a factory with a big smoke stack,

      D
And the smoke came out so billowy and black.

      G
It blew out the top and it blew up high.

It blew all over in the clear blue sky.

Verse 2:

G
Then more factories came into town.

      D
And the cars were driving all around.

      G
The air got gritty and not so clear,

And the people all said it sure stinks around here.

Chorus:

```
    G           C               G           D
        Everywhere  it's    the    same   old    air.

            G       C           G       D
    It's  the  same air  everywhere   that we   all   share.

    G           C               G           D
        Everywhere  it's    the    same   old    air

                G
    It's   the   same   air   everywhere   that we   all   share.
```

Verse 3:

```
    G
    The   people  got   together  both   the   old   and   the   young.

                D
    And   they   said   "We've   gotta   protect   our   lungs.
    G
    We've   gotta   lot   of   work   that's   gotta   be   done.

                                    D       G
    Let's   lean   on   the   people   in   Washington."
    G
    So   they   all   worked   together   and   they   told   the   facts,
            D
    They   got   a   law   passed   called   the   Clean   Air   Act.

            G
    If   you   make   it   dirty,   then   you've   gotta   clean   it   up.
                                        D       G
    And   you   can't   use   the   sky   for   a   garbage   dump.
```

Repeat Chorus:

Verse 4:

```
    G
    I've   got   a   neighbor   who   burns   big   fires.

            D
    He   burns   his   leaves   and   he   burns   his   tires.
    G
    I   went   over   to   talk   one   day.
                                D       G
    Now   he's   doing   it   a   better   way.
```

G
He takes his tires to an old junk lot.
  D
He puts his leaves on his garden plot.
G
The soil gets richer and so does he.

And everybody's happier, even me.

Chorus:
G   C   G   D
   Everywhere it's the same old air.

         G   C   G   D
It's the same air everywhere that we all share.

G   C   G   D
   Everywhere it's the same old air

            G
It's the same air everywhere that we all share.

It's the same air everywhere that we all share.

It's the same air everywhere that we all share.

HELP KEEP IT CLEAN

a round to the tune of "Fish and Chips and Vinegar"

Capo 3rd Fret
Starting Pitch: Open 3rd string

Words and Music by
KRISTIN ALBRIGHT, FELICIA AYALA, MICHELLE DOMINGUEZ,
TEKOA CHILCOTE and JESSICA BARON

Standard Chords:

G   D

GITC Chords:

G   D

Beginning Strum:

Intermediate Strum:

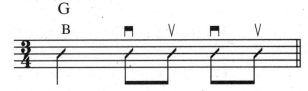

Part 1:

G
For the world, plant a tree,

D   G
Plant a tree, plant a tree.

G
For the world, plant a tree,

D   G
Keep the air clean.

G
Don't chop the trees in our rainforest.

D   G
Our rainforest, our rainforest,

G
Don't chop the trees in our rainforest,

D   G
Keep the air clean.

Part 2:

G
Don't dump your trash in our ocean,

D   G
Our ocean, our ocean.

G
Don't dump your trash in our ocean,

D   G
Keep our waves clean.

G
Don't spill your oil in our ocean,

D   G
Our ocean, our ocean.

G
Don't spill your oil in our ocean,

D   G
Keep our waves clean.

Part 3:

G
One newspaper, one soda can,

G
One plastic bottle, one milk jug,

G   D   G
One juice carton, one glass bottle, recycling's good!

Unison Ending:

G
Our great earth is our

D   G
Home, one and only.

G
So please do your part

          D   G
And help keep it clean!

Chapter 5
Every Living Thing

By Steve Van Zandt

I can't really talk about animals without talking about my sister. I'm not saying that I think of my sister as an animal, no, in fact, I'm the little brother so I was the family's little mischievous monkey or huggable teddy bear. If my sister had a superhero power it would be the one that lets her relate so well with animals. Right now she cares for 24 llamas, 6 goats, 3 dogs, 2 cats and a rooster that someone gave her, whom she calls "Doodle Do." Plus, she raises bees, three hives in fact.

It was the same way growing up. People, knowing of my sister's superhero powers, would often give her a stray or hurt animal. One time some friends delivered a baby grey squirrel that they saw fall out of a tree. Using her doll's baby bottle filled with milk and honey and an inverted coon-skin cap for a bed, (in those days we loved stories about Daniel Boone), she nursed Jo Jo the Squirrel back to life. She named him after her boyfriend. Jo Jo became our pet squirrel but not one that lived in a cage; Jo Jo lived freely in our backyard. When we came out in the morning, Jo Jo would come down from that twisted old plumb tree and nibble peanuts from our hands and then climb up one of us to sit on the top of our head.

Now I know that one should never give human food to wild animals because it makes them pests and ultimately is worse for the animal. But Jo Jo was different because he imprinted on my sister and believed we were his kin. Good kin we were, for we never held any restraints for Jo Jo to discover who he was. My sister says that he found a girl squirrel and she probably heard him say goodbye. For the rest of us he just disappeared. Thanks to Jo Jo, I look at squirrels today with playful fascination. I like to chase them up a tree running around and around as they spiral up the tree. I love their branch-to-branch acrobatics and the way they stand still and twitch that fluffy tail.

I discovered that just like the stereotypes about people, we can hold stereotypes about animals. As a kid I loved stories about Curious George and wished that I had a monkey for a friend. When someone gave my sister a spider monkey, I realized that wild animals were best in the wild. Gone were my images of funny monkeys peeling bananas. This guy would bite down sideways, eating the peel and often leaving the actual banana. Where he was caged, all the leaves from off of the morning glories were stripped bare from their vines. When you came close you could see his strength and feel his wildness. When we found someone who would take him and hopefully give him a home with more space, we had to give him a sleeping pill in order to move him safely. I realized that it's best to see animals in their natural habitat and to know that those habitats are being preserved.

From squirrels to monkeys, bees, birds and bears, animals make our lives complete. We are deeply intertwined in ways that we are just now discovering. Our existence depends upon a knowledgeable and respectful kinship with animals.

There's one more thing that I need to mention about my sister. She can sing to animals so that they understand her. You see, she has an old dog that she needs to give a pill to every night. So while she is making her goat cheese she rolls the pill up in a cheese ball. Now in the interest of fairness she makes three cheese balls so none of the dogs will feel left out. Then she sings, "Cheeseballs cheeseballs for everyone. For cheeseballs cheeseballs doggies run." No matter where they are, those doggies come running in and they sit as politely as can be with big cheesy grins.

How We Can Make a Difference

1. Be kind to the animals in your life. Ask yourself if they are getting everything they need on a daily basis. If you need to do a little more to make their lives better, go for it.

2. Observation is the key to understanding what animals are feeling. They communicate with each other using their own language, just like we use ours. For example, at first glance it can be hard to tell if two dogs are playing or fighting with each other. Play barks are often higher-pitched than fear or warning barks, and noticing their eyes and tail position can help you understand their intentions. Listen, observe, and learn.

3. Step into the animal's "shoes." Try and imagine what it would be like walking twenty miles every day to find food for your family, or how it would feel to get stuck in a tangle of plastic that is much stronger than you are. Thinking like this can help us understand our environment and the animals that reside within it.

4. Find out about volunteering at your local animal shelter or animal rescue organization. Many have programs for young people, and some offer summer opportunities to socialize animals and learn to take care of them.

5. Adopt a pet. You can save animals that need homes; it's easy to do. Many pet stores host adoption days, and the local pound has always been a great place to find a puppy, dog, cat, or bunny. There are even rescue groups for dogs by breed. For instance, if you know you want a Golden Retriever, search online under "Golden Retriever Rescue." When you decide, make sure you are ready to give the animal the proper care it needs to live a happy life.

6. Learn about the movement to reduce the number of unwanted cats in urban communities through spay & neuter programs. You can find out more about this through your local SPCA.

7. Live and let live, and learn about "Have a Heart Traps." Not all wild animals in your backyard are friendly; sometimes they need help getting back to the woods. You can learn to capture these animals humanely so they don't suffer needlessly.

8. Find the right animal control agency that will go the extra mile to relocate squirrels, skunks, raccoons, beavers, possums, rats, snakes, and others. They know all about moving wild animals, and how to do it safely.

9. Know who your local wild animal rescue heroes are. This way, when you find an injured animal, you'll know exactly who to call for help. It's great to be prepared, and the sooner you can get the animal help, the better chance it has of surviving.

10. If you live in an area where people are raising farm animals such as goats, pigs, sheep, cows, horses, or llamas, take a field trip and ask lots of questions. This will give you an opportunity to make a connection with the farmer, the animals, and discover your own response to being around the animals. Some people find that they have a particular bond with one kind of animal, which can become a passionate form of care and service throughout a lifetime. Who knows, maybe you are a horse whisperer!

11. Give thought to your diet. Consider the wellbeing of animals when you choose what you eat. This can mean giving up eating certain kinds of meat, or eating meat that comes from animals that have been raised and slaughtered humanely. Deciding what you do and don't eat is a completely personal decision each one of us makes for ourselves.

Knowledge is Power: Where to Learn More

Books

- *National Geographic Wild Animal Atlas*
- *National Geographic Encyclopedia of Animals*
- *How to Heal a Broken Wing*, by Bob Graham
- *Panda Bear, Panda Bear, What Do You See?*, by Bill Martin, and Eric Carle
- *Moon Bear*, by Brenda Z. Guiberson and Ed Young
- *All Creatures Great and Small*: The Complete Collection, by James Herriott

Organizations

- National Wildlife Federation; www.nwf.org
- The Wildlife Conservation Society; www.wcs.org
- The National Audubon Society; conservation.audubon.org
- The Association of Zoos and Aquariums; www.aza.org
- International Bird Rescue Research Center; www.ibrrc.org
- The Marine Mammal Center; www.marinemammalcenter.org
- Living Free Animal Sanctuary; www.living-free.org
- The World Wildlife Fund; www.worldwildlife.org

Websites

- Defenders of Wildlife's Kids Page; www.kidsplanet.org
- US Fish and Wildlife Service, Endangered Species Program; www.fws.gov/endangered
- Audubon Society's Kids Page; www.audubon.org/educate/kids
- Green People, website listing many humane societies, adoption centers and rescue orgs by state; www.greenpeople.org/humanesociety.htm
- How to Start a Non-Profit Animal Rescue Organization; www.ehow.com/how_2117271_start-nonprofit-animal-rescue.html
- Bill's Wildlife Sites, a long and current list of great organizations; www.wildlifer.com/wildlifesites/nonprofit.html
- The Wildlife Conservation Society Saving Wildlife Page; www.wcs.org/saving-wildlife.aspx

Find these and many more helpful website addresses at www.greensongbook.com.

58

EVERY LIVING THING

Capo: None
Starting Pitch: Open 2nd string

Words and Music by
ROD MACDONALD

Standard Chords:

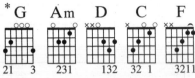

*The chords in this song go beyond the basic GITC chord fingerings.
Either use the standard tuning chords for this song,
or feel free to use the suggested, more advanced Open G tuning chords.

GITC Chords:

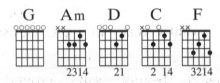

Beginning Strum:

Intermediate Strum 1:

Intermediate Strum 2:

Advanced Strum: Travis Pick

Verse 1:

G   Am
Seems like there ought to be a way

D   G
    to look each other in the eye.

                                    Am
To see we're all in this together and

D   G
Put all thoughts of victory aside.

C   F   C
    Seems like there ought to be a way to

G   D
    turn some fear into trust.

G   C   G   C
No matter what you say, there has to be a way,

        D   G
Every living thing is counting on us.

Verse 2:
```
G                                      Am
Seems  like  there  ought  to  be  a  way
      D                          G
to    separate  freedom  from  the  flag,
                                 Am
To    see   what's  real  in  the  illusion.
      D                              G
Sometimes  a  beauty  walks  around  in  rags.
C             F           C
Seems  like  there  ought  to  be  agreement,
G                                D
we  would  rather  live  in  peace  than  fight.
G             C        G        C
No  matter  what  you  say,  there  has  to  be  a  way,
      D                      G
Every  living  thing  is  on  our  side.
```

Verse 3:
```
G                                      Am
Seems  like  if  there's  a  god  in  heaven
      D                          G
We  must've  been  put  here  to  get  along,
                                 Am
To  see  that  life  is  for  the  living,
      D                              G
To  leave  alive  the  living  when  we're  done.
C             F           C
Seems  like  this  ship  out  on  the  ocean
      G                          D
Must  fly  on  the  wings  of  the  dove.
      G             C        G        C
No  matter  what  you  say,  there  has  to  be  a  way,
      D                      G
Every  living  thing  is  reason  enough.
      G             C        G        C
No  matter  what  you  say,  there  has  to  be  a  way,
      D                          G
Every  living  thing  is  counting  on  us.
```

UNDER ONE SKY

Capo: None
Starting Pitch: 3rd fret, 2nd string

Words and Music by
RUTH PELHAM

Standard Chords:

GITC Chords:

Beginning Strum:

Intermediate Strum:

Chorus:

          G   C
We're   all   a   family   under   one   sky.

               D   G
We're   a   family   under   one   sky.

          G   C
We're   all   a   family   under   one   sky.

               D   G
We're   a   family   under   one   sky.

Verse 1:

                       C   G
Well,   we're   plumbers,   we're   doctors,

             D   G
We're   farmers   and   teachers   too.

                       C   G
Well,   we're   plumbers,   we're   doctors,

             D   G
We're   farmers   and   teachers   too.

Repeat Chorus:

Verse 2:

                       C   G
Well,   we're   lions,   we're   elephants,

             D   G
We're   puppies   and   kangaroos.

                       C   G
Well,   we're   lions,   we're   elephants,

             D   G
We're   puppies   and   kangaroos.

Repeat Chorus:

Verse 3:

                      C   G
Well,   we're daisies, we're tulips,

                  D   G
We're roses,   chrysanthemums.

                      C   G
Well,   we're daisies, we're tulips,

                  D   G
We're roses, chrysanthemums.

Verse 4:

                 C   G
We're   Americans, we're Russians,

                 D   G
We're   Italians and   Vietnamese.

                 C   G
We're   Israelis, we're Irish,

                 D   G
We're   Africans and we're   Chinese.

Repeat Chorus:

EARTH SONG

Capo 3rd Fret
Starting Pitch: Open 3rd string

Words and Music by
PETER ALSOP

Standard Chords:

GITC Chords:

Beginning Strum:

This song can be sung as a round.
When one group completes singing the first four lines,
the second group begins.

Verse 1:

```
    G       D           G   D
Our song starts with  a   child's birth.
    G         Em    C        D
We're taught that people rule  the  earth.
    G      D     G        D
But every creature has  a   song
     G        Em     D       G
That we  can't hear if  we're too  strong
    C       G        D      Em
For those with paws and fins and wings
    C                   D
Each knows the  song its  family sings.
    Em                C
The wind, the  river, trees and  clouds
    G                 D    G
Cannot be   heard if  we're too  loud!!
```

Chorus:

```
    G   D     G   D
All together, open  hearts,
    G  Em       C         D
In  harmony we  sing  our  parts.
    G        D     G   D
When all  of  nature sings along,
    G        Em    C    G
Then we  can  hear our  Earth song.
```

```
G        D      G      D
All   together, open  hearts,
    G     Em       C          D
In   harmony  we   sing   our   parts.
      G           D      G     D
When all   of   nature  sings  along,

      G      Em       C       G
Then  we  can  hear  our  Earth  song.
```

Verse 2:

```
G        D       G          D
Rabbit, Clover,  Owl   and   Bee,

G       Em          C             D
Redtail Hawk  and   Great  Salt  Sea.

G          D        G       D
Mountain Lion,  Thunderstorm,

G       Em      D         G
Redwood, Cactus, Rice  and  Corn.
C       G      D        Em
Raven, Spider, Crab  and   Snail,

C               D
Catfish, Heron, Pond  and   Whale.

Em                  C
Pine  Tree, Jaybird, Wind  and  Moose,

G                D        G
Bear  and  Otter, Wolf  and  Goose.
```

Verse 3:

```
G   D       G  D
Kangaroo  and    Manatee,

G      Em         C        D
Cobra, Shark  and  Chimpanzee.

G        D         G      D
Butterfly,     Volcano,  Moss

G     Em     D  G
Turtle, Beetle, Albatross
C     G      D        Em
Dove,  Giraffe, Gazelle, Baboon,

C               D
Snake, Gorilla, Mouse, Racoon

Em                  C
Rose   and   Tiger,  Porpoise,  Ant,

G        D  G
Buffalo  and   Elephant.
```

Verse 4:

      G   D   G   D
The   promise that a   sunrise brings

      G   Em   C   D
Is one more chance to   dance and   sing.

      G   D   G   D
The   child helps the grown-up   see

      G   Em   D G
We   need more balance musically.

      C   G   D   Em
So   every creature, raise your   voice.

      C   D
Each holy day we   all   rejoice

      Em   C
And   celebrate how we   survive

      G   D   G
The   Earth song is our song of life

Chorus:

G   D   G   D
All   together, open   hearts,

G Em   C   D
In harmony we   sing our   parts.

      G   D   G   D
When all   of   nature sings along,

G   Em   D G
Then we   hear our Earth song.

G   D   G   D
All   together, open   hearts,

G Em   C   D
In harmony we   sing our   parts.

      G   D   G   D
When all   of   nature sings along,

G   Em   D G
Then we   hear our Earth song.

BRING BACK THE BAT

Capo 3rd Fret
Starting Pitch: Open 2nd string

Words by NANCY SCHIMMEL
Music by FRAN AVNI

Standard Chords:

GITC Chords:

Beginning Strum:

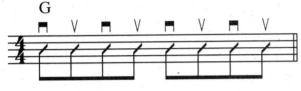

Intermediate Strum:

Advanced Strum:

Verse 1:

G
We wake up when the bat goes to bed.
D
Don't ban the bat, don't ban the bat.
    G   C
He sleeps with his feet up over his head.
        G D   G
Oh, bring back the bat.

Verse 2:

G
He flies like a bird but he's more like a mouse.
D
Don't ban the bat, don't ban the bat.
    G   C
He can't build a nest so build him a house.
      G D   G
Oh, bring back the bat.

Bridge:

C
Bring the bat back for the balance of nature.

G
Bring the bat back to the banks of the stream.

C
Bring the bat back, there's a bat in your future.

      D
Be a bat girl or a bat boy on the bat's home team.

Verse 3:

G
Birds eat mosquitos and so does the bat.
D
Don't ban the bat, don't ban the bat.
  G   C
Mosquitos eat me and I don't like that.
      G   D   G
Oh, bring back the bat.

Verse 4:

G
Build the bat a box and she'll catch a batch of bugs.
D
Don't ban the bat, don't ban the bat.
G   C
Raise little bats and give them little bat hugs.
      G   D   G
Oh, bring back the bat.

Verse 5:

G
Bats aren't bad, they're bashful and sweet.
D
Don't ban the bat, don't ban the bat.
      G   C
They pollinate bananas for us to eat.
      G   D   G
Oh, bring back the bat.

Repeat Bridge:

Verse 6:

G
We wake up when the bat goes to bed.
D
Don't ban the bat, don't ban the bat.
      G   C
He sleeps with his feet up over his head.
      G   D   G
Oh, bring back the bat.
      G   D   G
Oh, bring back the bat.
      G   D   G
Oh, bring back the bat.

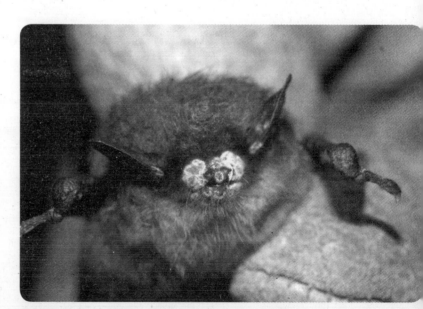

Little brown bat; close-up of nose with fungus, New York, Oct. 2008.
Credit: Photo courtesy Ryan von Linden/New York Department of Environmental Conservation

DOLPHINS, DOLPHINS IN THE SEA
Sung to the tune of "Twinkle, Twinkle, Little Star"

Capo 3rd Fret
Starting Pitch: Open 3rd string

Words and Music by
JESSICA BARON

Standard Chords:

GITC Chords:

Beginning Strum:

Intermediate Strum:

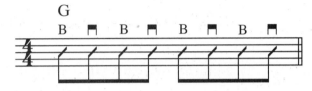

Verse 1:

G   C   G
Dolphins, dolphins in the sea,

C   G   D   G
Swim forever wild and free.

G   C   G   D
Through the waves you arch and dive!

G   C   G   D
In a pod of three four five!

G   C   G
Dolphins, dolphins in the sea,

C   G   D   G
Swim forever wild and free.

Verse 2:

G   C   G
Dolphins, dolphins in the sea,

C   G   D   G
Sing your playful songs for me!

G   C   G   D
Circling, circling all around,

G   C   G   D
Each one makes a joyful sound.

G   C   G
Dolphins, dolphins in the sea,

C   G   D   G
Swim forever wild and free.

Verse 3:

G   C   G
Dolphins, dolphins in the sea,

C   G   D   G
You are mammals just like me.

G   C   G   D
Bottlenose, Orca, White - Sided, Spinner,

G   C   G   D
Hunting fish and squid for dinner!

G   C   G
Dolphins, dolphins in the sea,

C   G   D   G
Swim forever wild and free.

C   G   D   G
Swim forever wild and free.

I WILL BE YOUR FRIEND

Capo 5th Fret
Starting Pitch: Open 4th string

Words and Music by
GUY DAVIS

Standard Chords:

GITC Chords:

Beginning Strum:

Advanced Strum (Travis Pick):

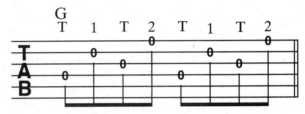

Verse 1:

G
If you've got troubles and you need a helping hand,

C   G
If you've got troubles and you need a helping hand,

Em   D   G   C
If you've got troubles and you need a helping hand,

      G   D G
Come to me and I will be your friend.

Chorus:

D   G   C   G
I will be your friend, yeah, I will be your friend.

Em   D   G   C
If you've got troubles and you need a helping hand,

      G   D G
Come to me and I will be your friend.

Verse 2:

G
If you are hungry and you've got no place to stay,

C   G
If you are hungry and you've got no place to stay,

Em   D   G   C
If you are hungry and you've got no place to stay,

      G   D G
Come to me and I will be your friend.

Repeat Chorus:

Verse 3:

G
If   you   are   lonely   and   you've   got   nobody   to   love,

C   G
If   you   are   lonely   and   you've   got   nobody   to   love,

Em   D   G   C
If   you   are   lonely   and   you've   got   nobody   to   love,

                          G   D   G
Come   to   me   and   I   will   be   your   friend.

Chorus:

D   G   C   G
I   will   be   your   friend, yeah,   I   will   be   your   friend.

Em   D   G   C
If   you've   got   troubles   and   you   need   a   helping   hand,

                          G   D   G   C
Come   to   me   and   I   will   be   your   friend.

                          G   D   G   C   G
Come   to   me   and   I   will   be   your   friend.

Chapter 6
Farm to Table

by Caprice Potter

My name is Caprice Potter and I am the director of Life Lab Science at Gateway School in Santa Cruz, California where I teach kindergarten through eighth grade science in a quarter acre garden classroom. Our program has garnered a Sustainability Award and is certified as a School Yard Habitat through the National Wildlife Federation. I am dedicated to providing children with opportunities to understand where food comes from and how to grow it as well as how prepare it! I want to help children to understand the science of sustainable farming and to become passionate stewards of the earth.

It's good in this day and age to understand where everything that we consume comes from and how it gets to us so that we can make really wise choices. The nutritional aspect of our life lab program is crucial. When we grow our own food, we tend to love it, eat it, and get the full nutritional benefit of eating fresh-picked herbs, fruits and vegetables. Children here do a lot of tasting in the garden. They compare the flavors of various foods, their palates develop, and their bodies grow healthier! They develop life sustaining knowledge and skills that will last them into adulthood when they will become the standard bearers and food growers, the marketers and consumers of our culture. Falling in love with the earth and allowing that love to stir a desire to protect our planet is what I want students everywhere to gain from having daily experiences in a living laboratory!

How We Can Make A Difference

1. Do what people have done in school for decades: Plant a lima bean in a clear container with drainage so you can see the parts of the plant as they emerge. Guess what you will see first! Reference the link: http://www.ehow.com/how_2223122_grow-lima-beans-jar.html

2. The first life lab started with big truck tires filled with soil on pavement. Talk about a great way to reuse a tire! You, too, can put in a tire garden filled with vegetables or a window box filled with edible flowers so you can grow food where you can watch what happens.

3. If you notice predators on your vegetables, do not immediately resort to using a chemical cure to stop them. Find the natural way that makes the bad bugs go away and the good bugs stay. For example, exclude the ants from your fruit trees so they won't keep the good bugs away. When the ants are gone, then good bugs can move in to eat more bad bugs such as aphids! You can send the ants away from the fruit trees by using Tanglefoot, a substance made with castor oil and vegetable wax, and contains nothing toxic at all.

4. Plant a garden you can cook from such as a pasta garden or a salsa garden. Grow the things you love to taste!

5. Grow a medicinal garden that contains the herbs we can easily research for their medicinal benefits. Make teas and tinctures, lip balm, salve, and nice smelling lotions for a healthy body all over.

6. Learn about the nutrient cycle and the resource cycle and start a school-wide composting and recycling system where kids are in charge of picking up lunch scraps and bringing them to compost piles. Children are responsible for picking up, sorting, and delivering plastic, glass, and paper to the recycling area.

7. Learn about what makes healthy soil and get your soil ready to grow good food! You can use a soil test kit to learn about the NPK Nitrogen Phosphorus Potassium, learn what the soil needs to create nutritious plants and make sure you feed the soil so you can feed yourself.

8. When you shop for fruits and vegetables, do your best to go to your local farmers so you can buy from the organic or chemical free farmers. You will get food that was picked that morning so it's better for you, and your dollars will support local, family farmers who are using the highest quality seed and supplements to make the food.

9. If you cannot shop at a farmer's market, look for organic food at your grocery store and if there is not enough, ask the market manager to bring in more.

10. Eat healthy on purpose! Read the labels of what you are thinking about putting into your mouth and watch out for hidden unhealthy ingredients such as high fructose corn syrup! This adds calories, has no nutritional value and has probably been grown from bio-engineered seeds.

Knowledge is Power: Where to Learn More

Books

- *The Green Truck Garden Giveaway: a Neighborhood Story and Almanac,* by Jacqueline Briggs Martin and Alec Gillman
- *In Defense of Food: an Eater's Manifesto,* by Michael Pollan
- *The Growing Classroom: Garden-based Science,* by Roberta Jaffe and Gary Appel
- *The Lorax,* by Dr. Seuss
- *Smart by Nature: Schooling for Sustainability,* by Michael K. Stone
- *Life Lab Science Curriculum* (online book materials), http://www.lifelab.org

Organizations

- Life Lab Science Curriculum; http://www.lifelab.org
- Jane Goodall's Roots & Shoots; http://www.rootsandshoots.org
- Ecology Action; http://www.ecoact.org
- Seeds of Change; http://www.seedsofchange.com
- Botanical Interests; http://www.botanicalinterests.com
- Renee's Garden Seeds; http://www.reneesgarden.com

Websites

- Center for Ecoliteracy; http://www.ecoliteracy.org
  The Center for Ecoliteracy is a public foundation dedicated to education for sustainable living.
- National Gardening Association; http://www.garden.org
  Nonprofit provider of plant-based education aims to promote home, school, and community gardening.
- Kids Gardening; http://www.kidsgardening.com
  Kids Gardening explores gardening resources for family, teachers, and beginner or experienced gardeners.
- Acorn Naturalists; http://www.acornnaturalists.com
  Science and environmental education supplies for teachers, outdoor educators, interpreters, homeschools, camp leaders, naturalists, nature centers and more.
- Beyond Pesticides; http://www.beyondpesticides.org/
  Beyond Pesticides (formerly National Coalition Against the Misuse of Pesticides) works with allies in protecting public health and the environment to lead the transition to a world free of toxic pesticides.

Find these and many more helpful website addresses at www.greensongbook.com.

TWO-FIELD FARM

Capo 5th Fret
Starting Pitch: Open 3rd string

Words and Music by
NANCY SCHIMMEL

Standard Chords:

G   C   D

21 3   32 1   132

GITC Chords:

G   C   D

2 14   21

Beginning Strum:

G

Intermediate Strum:

G
B

Advanced Strum:

G
B

Verse 1:

G
Two-Field Farm's a good old farm, two field farm's a wonder.

C   D   G
Feeds two farmers and their kids and a big black horse named Thunder.

C   D   G
Feeds two farmers and their kids and a big black horse named Thunder.

Verse 2:

G
One field's for the farmers, this field is full of wheat.

C   D   G
The farmers grow the wheat to make the daily bread they eat.

C   D   G
The farmers grow the wheat to make the daily bread they eat.

Verse 3:

G
One field's for the big black horse who helps them plow the ground.

C   D   G
And every several years or so they trade those fields around.

C   D   G
And every several years or so they trade those fields around.

74

Verse 4:

G
The horse's field is clover, it gives a double yield.

                           C   D   G
The clover feeds the horse, of course, but also feeds the field.

                           C   D   G
The clover feeds the horse, of course, but also feeds the field.

Verse 5:

G
'Cause about a million critters live on each clover's roots.

                   C   D   G
And they are fixing nitrogen right underneath your boots.

                   C   D   G
And they are fixing nitrogen right underneath your boots.

Verse 6:

G
The nitrogen's not broken, it's just that it's alone.

                  C   D   G
They fix it up with minerals, that's how good soil is grown.

                  C   D   G
They fix it up with minerals, that's how good soil is grown.

Verse 7:

G
And when the soil is rich, the farmers plow it up for wheat

                                  C   D   G
And thank the nitrogen - fixing bacteria when they eat,

                               C   D   G
And thank the nitrogen - fixing bacteria when they eat.

Repeat Verse 1:

DIRT MADE MY LUNCH

Capo 1st Fret
Starting Pitch: Open 2nd string

Words and Music by
STEVE VAN ZANDT
with the BANANA SLUG STRING BAND

Standard Chords:

GITC Chords:

Beginning Strum:

Intermediate Strum:

Chorus:

```
G                    C         G
Dirt made my lunch, dirt made my lunch,

C              G
Thank you dirt, thanks a bunch,

            C                                G
For my salad, my sandwich, my milk and my munch 'cuz

D                  G
Dirt, you made my lunch.

D                  G
Dirt, you made my lunch.
```

Verse 1:

```
Em                    G
Dirt is a word we often use

         Em                      G
When we're talkin' about that earth beneath our shoes.

         Em                  G
It's a place where plants can sink their toes,

         C                   D
And in a little while a garden grows.
```

Repeat Chorus:

Verse 2:

Em   G
A   farmer's plow will   tickle the   ground

                            Em   G
You know the earth has laughed when the wheat is   found.

Em   G
The   grain is   taken and the   flour is   ground,

              C   D
For   making a   sandwich to   munch on   down.

Repeat Chorus:

Verse 3:

        Em   G
A   stubby green beard grows upon the   land

Em   G
Out of   the   soil the   grass will   stand.

        Em   G
But   under hoof it   must bow,

        C   D
For   making milk by   way of   a   cow.

Chorus:

G   C   G
Dirt made my   lunch, dirt   made my   lunch,

C   G
Thank you dirt, thanks a   bunch,

          C   G
For my salad, my sandwich, my   milk and my munch 'cuz

D   G
Dirt, you   made my   lunch.

        D   G   C   G
Yeah, dirt, you   made my   lunch.

MY ROOTS GO DOWN

Capo 7th Fret
Starting Pitch: Open 4th string

Words and Music by
SARAH PIRTLE

Standard Chords:

GITC Chords:

Beginning Strum:

Intermediate Strum:

Advanced Strum (Travis pick):

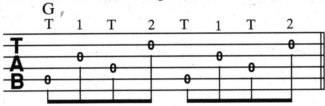

Chorus:

G
My roots go down, down to the earth,

                C   G
My roots go down, down to the earth,

                                         Em
My roots go down, down to the earth,

        D   C   G
My roots go down.

Verse 1:

G
I am an ancient redwood tree, *oak* *at school*

                    C *oak*   G
I am an ancient redwood tree, *at school*

                  oak   Em
I am an ancient redwood tree, *at school*

        D   C   G
My roots go down.

Repeat Chorus:

Verse 2:

G
I   am   a   sunflower reaching   for   the   sun.
                      C   G
I   am   a   sunflower reaching   for   the   sun.
                                            Em
I   am   a   sunflower reaching   for   the   sun.
      D   C   G
My   roots   go   down.

Verse 3:

G
I   am   a   cornstalk   tall   and   strong.
                        C   G
I   am   a   cornstalk   tall   and   strong.
                                          Em
I   am   a   cornstalk   tall   and   strong.
      D   C   G
My   roots   go   down.

Repeat Chorus:

Verse 4:

G
I   am   a   wind - blown dandelion,
                        C   G
I   am   a   wind - blown dandelion,
                                          Em
I   am   a   wind - blown dandelion,
      D   C   G
My   roots   go   down.

Verse 5:

G
I   am   every   living   thing,
                        C   G
I   am   every   living   thing,
                                          Em
I   am   every   living   thing,
      D   C   G
My   roots   go   down.

Repeat Chorus:

EVERY THIRD BITE

Capo 3rd Fret
Starting Pitch: Open 4th string

Words by NANCY SCHIMMEL
Music by JUDY FJELL

Standard Chords:

G   D   C   G7

GITC Chords:

G   D   C   G7

Beginning Strum (Shuffle):

Intermediate Strum (Reggae):

Verse 1:

G   D
For every third bite you eat, thank the bees,

                                                 G   G7
For the peppers on your pizza and the cheese.

        C
You know that bees make honey,

                G
But the nectar's just the tease,

        D   G   G7
For every third bite you eat, thank the bees.

Chorus:

C
Hum a little hum, (hmm)

G
Buzz a little buzz, (bzz),

        D   G   G7
For every third bite you eat, thank the bees.

C
Hum a little hum, (hmm)

G
Buzz a little buzz, (bzz),

        D   G
For every third bite you eat, thank the bees.

Verse 2:

G   D
Some plants send their pollen on the breeze,

                                                 G   G7
Pollen makes some people wheeze and sneeze.

C
Bees are so much neater,

                G
Toting pollen on their knees,

        D   G   G7
For every third bite you eat, thank the bees.

Repeat Chorus:

    Verse 3:

G   D
Flowers cannot go out on a date.

                                     G
They just have to sit around and wait.

  C
Until they get the pollen,

       G
They cannot set the seeds,

         D   G
For every third bite you eat, thank the bees.

    Verse 4:

G   D
For bees and moths and hummingbirds and bats

                          G   G7
The flowers all put out their welcome mats,

  C
The colors and the nectar

      G
And the smells are sure to please

    D   G   G7
The bats and moths and hummingbirds and bees.

Repeat Chorus:

    Verse 5:

G   D
It isn't every bee knows how to sting,

                         G   G7
Some are only sweetness on the wing.

      C
Like the Orange Blossom special,

    G
They sound among the trees.

    D   G   G7
For every third bite you eat, thank the bees.

Repeat Chorus:

    D   G   C   G
For every third bite you eat thank the bees.

JOHNNY APPLESEED

Capo: None
Starting Pitch: Open 2nd string

Words and Music by
STEVE GILLETTE

Standard Chords:

*G   D   C   Em   Em#7   Am

21 3   132   32 1   23   21   231

GITC Chords:

G   D   C   Em   Em#7   Am

21   2 14   2 4   2 4   2314

*The chords in this song go beyond the basic GITC chord fingerings.
Either use the standard tuning chords for this song,
or feel free to use the suggested, more advanced Open G tuning chords.

Beginning Strum:

Intermediate Strum:

Advanced Strum:

Chorus:

```
    G              D           C              G
Hey, Johnny Appleseed, you really are a friend indeed;

Em                     C            D
You left a path for me to follow, through the apple trees.

    G              D           C              G
Hey Johnny Appleseed, you taught me everything I need;

Em                     C              D       G
And I will follow where you lead, Johnny Appleseed.
```

Verse 1:

```
    G        D                    G
What a time to be alive, so early in the morning

            Em              C           G           D
And the warm fire of the summer sunrise sets the skies ablaze.

Em          Em#7            C             G
We wondered deep into the wilderness and back again,

C                   Am              D
A journey I'll remember 'til the end of my days.
```

Repeat Chorus:

Verse 2:
```
D                             G
Down  through  the  years,  nothing  really  changes.

Em                  C            G            D
Somewhere  deep  within  us  we're  the  same  as  we  were  then.

Em            Em#7     C                    G
If  I  could  see  you  comin'  through  the  meadow,

C                         Am            D
You  know  I'd  gladly  go   that  happy  way  with  you  again.
```

Chorus:
```
G           D           C                 G
Hey,  Johnny  Appleseed,  you  really  are  a  friend  indeed;

Em                  C            D
You  left  a  path  for  me  to  follow,  through  the  apple  trees.

G           D           C                 G
Hey  Johnny  Appleseed,  you  taught  me  everything  I  need;

Em                  C                D           G
And  I  will  follow  where  you  lead,  Johnny  Appleseed,
D         G
Johnny  Appleseed.
```

THE ZUCCHINI SONG

Capo: None
Starting Pitch: Open 2nd string

Words and Music by
DAN CROW

Standard Chords:

GITC Chords:

Beginning Strum:

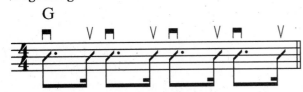

Intermediate Strum:

Chorus:

G
We have a garden,

I beg your pardon,

       C   G
We have a garden and we grow our own food.

We have a garden,

I beg your pardon,

  C   D   G
I didn't mean to shout and be so rude!

Verse 1:

G   C
We have some carrots and zucchini,

Lettuce and zucchini,

G
Tomatoes and zucchini and some peas.

        D
We have some cabbage and zucchini,

Onions and zucchini,

           G
Pepper and zucchini and some beans.

Verse 2:

G   C

We have some parsley and zucchini,

Broccoli and zucchini,

G

Mushrooms and zucchini and some greens.

 D

Alfalfa and zucchini,

Cauliflower and zucchini,

                                      G

Some celery and zucchini and some beans.

Repeat Chorus:

Verse 3: G   C

We have some berries and zucchini,

Melon and zucchini,

G

Pumpkin and zucchini and some bugs.

D

Spiders and zucchini,

Snails and zucchini,

                           G

Beetles and zucchini and some slugs.

Verse 4:

                  C

We have some popcorn and zucchini,

Ice cream and zucchini,

G

Pizza and zucchini and some kelp.

D

Candy and zucchini,

Chocolate and zucchini,

                          G

Zucchini, cchini, cchini, cchini, help!

Repeat Chorus:

    C   D   G

I didn't mean to shout and be so rude!

    C   D   G

I didn't mean to shout and be so rude!

THE GARDEN SONG

Capo 2nd Fret
Starting Pitch: Open 3rd string

Words and Music by
DAVID MALLETT

Standard Chords:

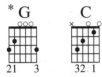

GITC Chords:

*The chords in this song go beyond the basic GITC chord fingerings.
 Either use the standard tuning chords for this song,
 or feel free to use the suggested, more advanced Open G tuning chords.

Beginning Strum:

Intermediate Strum:

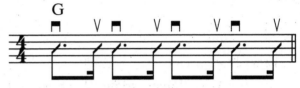

Advanced: Travis Pick

Chorus:

```
G            C        G
Inch  by  inch,  row  by   row,

C        D         G
Gonna  make  this  garden  grow.

C        D          G          Em
All  it  takes  is  a  rake  and  a  hoe,

       A               D
And  a  piece  of  fertile  ground.

G            C        G
Inch  by  inch,  row  by   row,

C        D              G
Someone  bless  these  seeds  I  sow.

       C        D          G       Em
Someone  warm  them  from  below  'til  the

A           D       G
Rains  come  tumbling  down.
```

Verse 1:

```
G                    C     G
Pullin'  weeds  and  pickin'  stones,

C        D         G
We  are  made  of  dreams  and  bones.

C        D         G       Em
Feel  the  need  to  grow  my  own,

       A               D
'Cause  the  time  is  close  at  hand.
```

```
G                    C        G
And  grain  for  grain,  sun  and  rain,
C          D        G
Find  my  way  in  nature's  chain.
        C         D    G       Em
And  tune  my  body  and  my  brain
          A       D       G
To    the  music  of  the  land.
```

Repeat Chorus:

Verse 2:

```
G                    C        G
Plant  your  rows  straight  and  long,
C        D           G
Temper  them  with  a  prayer  and  song.
C      D        G       Em
Mother  Earth  will  make  you  strong
          A                 D
If  you  give  her  loving  care.
G                    C  G
Old  crow  watching  hungrily
C        D        G
From  his  perch  in  yonder  tree.

C        D        G     Em
In   my  garden,  I'm  as  free
          A       D         G
As    that  feathered  thief  up  there.
```

Repeat Chorus:

Chapter 7
Reduce, Reuse, Recycle

by Jessica Anne Baron

My mother-in-law often used to exclaim with pride, "Use it up, wear it out, make it do, or do without!" A brilliant and stubborn New Englander, she made every item in her home earn its keep perpetually. Very little ever went to waste. Bare bones were simmered to make new broth. Clothing was refashioned. Left-over vegetables were frozen until enough of them amounted to ingredients for a "stewp" (combination soup and stew), and the house groaned under the weight of 100 year-old beds, first edition books, and 400 year-old heirlooms.

Mama took pride in thrift because it required more than frugality. It took Yankee creativity. She got on the recycling band wagon early, her back hallway becoming a dangerous obstacle course of bagged magazines, bottles, and cans years before any city waste management trucks ever delivered the recycle bins we take for granted.

Recycling is not new. It is a well-refined process that is very interesting. Not every city does it the same way. Do you know how your city does it? What exactly CAN you recycle and what do you WISH you could recycle? And once you've put something in the recycle bin, what happens to it? These are great questions to ask your local recycling service. You might be surprised at the answers. We could all use a little coaching from Mama these days.

David Morris of the Institute for Local Self-Reliance says, "The case for recycling is strong. The bottom line is clear. Recycling requires a trivial amount of our time. Recycling saves money and reduces pollution. Recycling creates more jobs than land-filling or incineration. And a largely ignored but very important consideration, recycling reduces our need to dump our garbage in someone else's backyard."

Here are some very interesting facts about recycling from the Oberlin College Resource Conservation Team at http://www.oberlin.edu/recycle/facts.html#plastic:

1. One dollar out of every $11.00 Americans spend for food goes for packaging—Styrofoam, plastic, paper, glass, and tin. We waste our money on needless packaging and waste our resources, too. If we recycle the packaging, things get better.

2. Styrofoam cannot be recycled. Each year Americans throw away 25,000,000,000 Styrofoam cups, enough to circle the earth 436 times! Do not take food home in Styrofoam containers or use Styrofoam products if you want to protect the earth.

3. Every year we make enough plastic film to shrink-wrap Texas. And Americans go through 25 billion plastic bottles every year. If every American household recycled just one out of every ten HDPE (high-density polyethylene) bottles they used, we'd keep 200 million pounds of the plastic out of landfills every year.

4. Every time a ton of steel is recycled, 2500 pounds of iron ore, 1000 pounds of coal and 40 pounds of limestone is preserved.

5. Every day Americans use enough steel and tin cans to make a steel pipe running from Los Angeles to New York—and back. And about 70% of all metal is used just once and is discarded. The remaining 30% is recycled. If we only recycle one-tenth of the cans we now throw away, we'd save about 3.2 billion of them every year. These days, the steel industry's annual recycling saves the equivalent energy to electrically power about 18 million households for a year. Imagine how much we could preserve if everyone did better.

How We Can Make A Difference

1. Let's Reduce! We can choose our clothing purchases thoughtfully, and avoid shopping for clothing we don't need but simply want because the clothing is "cool" and the brand is popular.

2. We can reduce the plastic we use by bringing cloth bags along when we go shopping. We can also take lunch to school in reusable containers and lunch boxes.

3. We can buy some foods in bulk to reduce the amount of packaging we use and throw away.

4. Let's Reuse! We can buy products in glass jars with good lids, then we can reuse those jars to store leftovers, craft supplies, or dry foods such as lentils and beans. Glass is a lot better for our environment than plastic. After all, it comes from nature—it used to be sand!

5. We can refashion our clothing by transforming one favorite "worn out" item into something wonderful! A shirt or dress becomes a one-of-a-kind bag, pillow, button covers, or patches!

6. Instead of buying water in plastic bottles and using more and more of them, we can carry our own high quality reusable water bottle (made with aluminum or other BPA-free products), filling it up as needed we reach a good water source.

7. Let's Recycle! We can ask our local recycling center exactly what we can recycle and what it will be turned into when they process it. Then we can recycle properly.

8. Pass our gently worn clothes along to others who will appreciate them. We can also bring our used clothing to any Patagonia store to donate it to the Common Threads program so the fibers can be made into new clothing!

9. When we must purchase drinks that come in plastic, glass, or paper containers, we can be sure always to recycle these containers at home when the beverages have been consumed. Let's keep our recyclables out of our trash cans!

10. We can "pitch in" when we are in public places such as parks and community events by noticing the recyclable containers others have left behind and pitch them into the correct recycling bins!

Knowledge is Power: Where to Learn More

Books

- *Beyond Recycling: A Re-user's Guide: 336 Practical Tips to save Money and Protect the Environment*, by Kathy Stein
- *Cradle to Cradle: Remaking the Way We Make Things*, by William McDonough and Michael Braungart
- *What's It Like, Living Green?: Kids Teaching Kids by the Way They Live*, by Jill Ammon Vanderwood and Emma Austin

Organizations

- Kokua Hawaii Foundation's Plastic Free Schools Program; www.kokuahawaiifoundation.org/plasticfreeschools

- Freecycle; http://www.freecycle.org/
  A worldwide gifting movement that reduces waste, saves precious resources and eases the burden on our landfills while enabling members to benefit from the strength of a larger community.

- BRING Recycling; http://www.bringrecycling.org/
  A broad-based organization offering positive, hands-on solutions to the serious environmental challenges of our time.

- Keep America Beautiful; http://www.kab.org/site/PageServer?pagename=index
  A practical approach that unites citizens, businesses and government to find solutions that advance the core issues of preventing litter, reducing waste, and beautifying communities.

Websites

- Earth 911; http://earth911.com/recycling/
  Guide to local resources including recycling centers, how to recycle, pollution prevention and how help protect the environment.

- The Global Recycling Network; http://www.grn.com/library/educational.htm
  Recycling Educational Resources. The following list points to various educational resources on the web that deal with recycling issues.

- Natural Resources Conservation's Service page about composting;
  http://www.nrcs.usda.gov/feature/backyard/compost.html

Find these and many more helpful website addresses at www.greensongbook.com.

THE THREE R'S (REDUCE, REUSE, RECYCLE)

(Adapted from the composition "Three Is A Magic Number")

Capo 5th Fret
Starting Pitch: Open, 2nd string

Music by BOB DOROUGH
Revised Lyrics by JACK JOHNSON

Standard Chords:

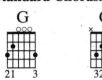

GITC Chords:

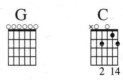

Beginning Strum:

Intermediate Strum:

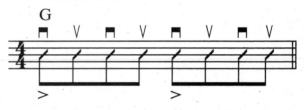

Advanced Strum:

Verse 1:

```
 G      C              G        C
Three,   it's  a  magic number
```

```
        G    C              G        C
Yes, it  is,       it's  a  magic number.
```

```
        G                    C
Because two  times  three  is   six,
```

```
      G                    C
And  three times six  is   eighteen,
```

```
        G                      C        G  C
And  the eighteenth letter  in  the  alphabet is  R.
```

```
          G    C                    G        C
We've  got three R's     we're going to  talk  about today.
```

```
We've got  to  learn  to...
```

90

Chorus:

    G   C
    Reduce, Reuse, Recycle.

    G   C
    Reduce, Reuse, Recycle.

    G   C
    Reduce, Reuse, Recycle.

    G   C
    Reduce, Reuse, Recycle.

Verse 2:

      G   C
    If you're going to the market to buy some juice,

         G
    You've got to bring your own bags and you

    C   G C
    Learn to reduce your waste.

         G C
    We got to learn to reduce.

       G   C
    And if your brother or your sister's got some cool clothes,

       G   C
    You could try them on before you buy some more of those.

     G C   G C
    Reuse, we gotta learn to reuse!

Bridge:

       G   C
    And if the first two R's don't work out,

         G
    And if you've got to make some trash,
    C
    Don't throw it out

     G C G
    Recycle, recycle, we've got to learn to...

Chorus:

        G   C
Reduce, Reuse, Recycle.

        G   C
Reduce, Reuse, Recycle.

        G   C
Reduce, Reuse, Recycle.

        G   C
Reduce, Reuse, Recycle.

             G   C   G   C
Because three,   it's a magic number

             G   C   G   C
Yes, it is,   it's a magic number.

Refrain:

G C G C G C G C
3   3   3   3

G   C
(3), 6   9   12 15

G   C
(3), 18 21 24 27

G   C
(3), 30 33 36

G   C
(3), 33 30 27

G   C
(3), 24 21 18

G   C
(3), 15 12 9   6   and

G C   G
(3),   it's a magic number.

GOOD GARBAGE

Capo 2nd Fret
Starting Pitch: 3rd fret, 2nd string

Words and Music by
TOM CHAPIN

Standard Chords:

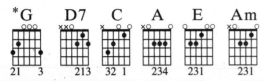

GITC Chords:

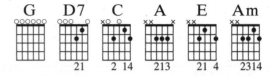

*The chords in this song go beyond the basic GITC chord fingerings.
Either use the standard tuning chords for this song,
or feel free to use the suggested, more advanced Open G tuning chords.

Beginning Strum:

Intermediate Strum:

Advanced Strum (Thumb-pluck):

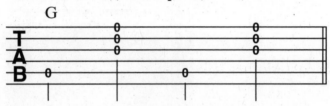

Verse 1:

G   D7
I had a turkey dinner, threw the bones away.

                                       G
They hauled them to the county dump without delay.

                                 C
By the following Thanksgiving, they had turned to clay.

        D7   G A D7
They're bio-de, bio-de, bio-degradable garbage.

Chorus:

G   D7
Good garbage breaks down as it goes,

                         G
That's why it smells bad to your nose.

             C
Bad garbage grows and grows and grows,

D7   G
Garbage is supposed to decompose.

Verse 2:

```
G                                        D7
Now,  styrofoam  is  bad,  it  lasts  a  thousand  years.
                                         G
A  packing  peanut's  born,  it  never  disappears.
                                              C
So  crumple  up  your  comics  when  you  ship  your  chandeliers,
      D7                              G A  D7
'Cause  comics  are  bio-de,  bio-degradable  garbage.
```

Repeat Chorus:

Bridge:

```
E
Every  time  that  we  buy  food,  we  also  buy  the  package.
                                              Am
Bottles,  boxes,  bags,  and  cans;  they  end  up  in  the  garbage.
D7                              G
Half  of  all  our  cash,  we're  spending  on  our  trash.
A                              D7
For  the  sake  of  Mother  Earth  let's  get  our  money's  worth!

Only  buy  bio-de,  bio-degradable...
```

Repeat Chorus 2 times:

```
         D7                              G
Yes,   garbage  is  supposed  to   decompose.
```

SOMEONE'S GONNA USE IT AFTER YOU

Capo 2nd fret
Starting Pitch: open 3rd string

Words and Music by
TOM CHAPIN

Standard Chords:

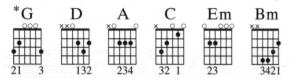

GITC Chords:

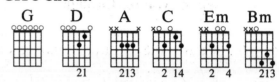

*The chords in this song go beyond the basic GITC chord fingerings.
Either use the standard tuning chords for this song,
or feel free to use the suggested, more advanced Open G tuning chords.

Beginning Strum:

Intermediate Strum:

Advanced Strum (Reggae):

Verse 1:

G
When you stand at the sink, did you ever think

                       D   G
About the water running down the drain?

That it used to be in the deep blue sea

        A   D
And before that it was rain.

          C   Em
Then it turned to snow for an Eskimo

   Bm   Em
To use in a snowball fight,

       A
Then it floated south 'til it reached your mouth

  D
To brush your teeth tonight.

Chorus:

C   G
Someone's gonna use it after you.

A
Someone needs that water

     D
When you're through.

    C   G
'Cause the water, land and air,

    C   G
These are things we've got to share.

C   D   C G C G
Someone's gonna use it after you.

Verse 2:

G
When you sneeze like thunder,

Did you ever wonder

     D G
If the air you set in motion

Might have helped to form a tropical storm

  A   D
Way out in the Western Ocean?

    C
Could have been blown out of

  Em
A blue whale's spout

    Bm   Em
As he dove beneath the seas.

  A
And now that air is in your care

    D
'Til you're finished with your Sneeze.

Chorus:

C   G
Someone's gonna use it, after you.

A
Someone needs to breathe it

    D
When you're through.

    C   G
'Cause the water, land and air,

    C   G
These are things we've got to share.

C   D   C G C G
Someone's gonna use it after you.

Bridge:

```
G           D                    G
Like  a   wheel,  the   world  is    turning,

            D                    G
Forest  green  and  sky   of    blue.

              Em                 A
It    will  turn  that  way  forever

                            D
As   the   old   is    born  anew...
```

Chorus:

```
C                            G
Someone's  gonna  use  it  after  you.

        A
So    leave  it  as  you'd  like  it

              D
When  you're  through.

            C              G
'Cause  the  water,  land  and  air,

            C              G
These  are  things  we've  got  to   share.

C              D          C   G   C   G
Someone's  gonna  use  it  after  you.
```

Repeat Chorus:

Chapter 8
A New Energy Path

by Andrew Revkin

Energy is vital to human well-being, enabling everything from reading homework at night to growing, moving and cooking food to fending off a winter freeze or summer heat wave to linking and educating communities via the Web. But the energy sources humans have relied on through recent centuries, from fossil fuels to firewood, can't possibly supply needs as populations crest somewhere near nine billion in the next few decades.

That's why, as a journalist and the Dot Earth blogger for The New York Times, I've written so much about the need for a sustained energy quest, from the kitchen light socket to the laboratory, the board room to the classroom to the Oval Office, in which the goal is a shift to a new relationship with this precious resource—conserving it as a normal part of daily life and engaging in a sustained push to advance science and technologies that can lead to new ways to light up human lives without overheating the planet or stripping its nonrenewable resources. You can learn more about my approach here at http://j.mp/eQuest

How We Can Make A Difference

1. If you can, move to a city or walkable town.
2. If you can't, think before you drive (plan trips to avoid coming and going).
3. Think before you toss and replace a possession, particularly something that took a lot of energy to manufacture.
4. Turn down the thermostat or turn off the A/C when you leave a house. The furniture doesn't care much about the temperature.
5. Insulate, insulate, and insulate some more.
6. Make nature your energy ally. Plant trees to cool things off. Shrink your lawn and replace it with something that doesn't require mowing or fertilizer (made with lots of energy).
7. Turn off the lights when you leave a room. The furniture doesn't notice.
8. Consider the energy that's required to move water and food when you make choices about these vital resources. The electricity needed to supply water to residents of southern California equals about a third of household electricity use in the area.
9. Convince your boss (or employees) to telecommute at least a couple of days a week.
10. Make something instead of buying something once in awhile.
11. If you're a student, consider shaping your career around the energy quest—whether by focusing on bringing electricity to poor places or finding ways to use it more efficiently in rich places.

Knowledge is Power: Where to Learn More

Places to Go

- Take the family to your local power source, whether it's run on coal, nuclear fuel, the wind or natural gas, to learn more about where that magical stuff coming out of a wall socket originates.

- If you live in a region that has an abundant source of energy, visit the source—whether a mine or oil field or dam or wind farm, to learn more about where that magical stuff coming out of a wall socket originates.

- If you're lucky enough to be able to travel abroad, visit a country where electricity is not taken for granted and learn how people cook, get around and light their homes.

- Visit your school and see if it has a program to cut its energy use. If it doesn't, help create one.

Books

- *The Carbon Age*, by Eric Roston
- *Energy: A Beginner's Guide*, by Vaclav Smil
- *Powering the Future*, by Daniel Botkin

Organizations

- American Council for an Energy-Efficient Economy; http://www.aceee.org/
- Americans for Energy Leadership; http://leadenergy.org/
- The Lumina Project; http://light.lbl.gov/
- Rural Energy Foundation; http://www.ruralenergy.nl/

Websites

- U.S. Department of Energy; www.energysavers.gov/
- Energy Guide, Smart Energy Choices; http://www.energyguide.com/
- Power Scorecard; http://powerscorecard.org/
- The New York Times; http://www.nytimes.com/energychallenge

Find these and many more helpful website addresses at www.greensongbook.com.

POWER

Capo 2nd Fret
Starting Pitch: 3rd fret, 2nd string

Words and Music by
JOHN and JOHANNA HALL

Standard Chords:

*G   C   Em   Am   Dm7   D

21 3   32 1   23   231   211   132

GITC Chords:

G   C   Em   Am   Dm7   D

2 14   2 4   2314   23   21

*The chords in this song go beyond the basic GITC chord fingerings.
Either use the standard tuning chords for this song,
or feel free to use the suggested, more advanced Open G tuning chords.

Beginning Strum:

G

Intermediate Strum:

G

Advanced Strum:

G
B

Chorus:

G   C   Em
Just give me the warm power of the sun.

             Am   C
Give me the steady flow of a waterfall.

       Dm7   F   C   G
Give me the spirit of living things as they return to clay.

                C   Em
Just give me the restless power of the wind.

            Am   C
Give me the comforting glow of a wood fire.

       Dm7   G   F   C
But please take all your atomic poison power away.

Verse 1:

G   C   Em
Everybody needs some power I'm told,

                   Am   C
To shield them from the darkness and the cold.

             Dm7   D
But some may see a way to take control
          F   C   G
When it's bought and sold.

```
              C                Em
I   know  that  lives  are  at  stake,
              Am                           C
Yours  and  mine  and  our  descendants  in  time.
                    Dm7                  D
There's  so  much  to  gain,  so  much  to  lose,
F                         G
Everyone  of  us  has  to  choose.
```

Repeat Chorus:

Verse 2:

```
G                  C              Em
We  are  only  now  beginning  to  see
              Am                       C
How  delicate  the  balance  of  nature  can  be.
            Dm7
The  limits  of  her  ways  have  been  defined
            F          C   G
And  we've  crossed  that  line.
                  C              Em
Some  don't  even  care  or  know  that  we'll  pay,
                  Am                     C
But  we  have  seen  the  face  of  death  in  our  day.
              Dm7                       D
There's  so  little  time  to  change  our  ways
            F        G
If  only  we  together  can  say...
```

Repeat Chorus:

FUTURE MAN FUTURE LADY

Capo 6th Fret
Starting Pitch: Open 2nd string

Words and Music by
ZIGGY MARLEY

Standard Chords:

GITC Chords:

Beginning Strum:

Intermediate Strum:

Verse 1:

```
  G        C          G
Future  Man  knows  what  to  do,

D                    G
He's  got  a  plan  to  help  this  land.

               C      G          D          G
He's  the  future  man,      he's  the  future  man.

             C     G
Future  Lady's  confident,

D                    G
She  knows  how  to  take  a  stand.

             C        G          D      G
She's  the  future  lady,      she's  the  future  lady.
```

Chorus 1:

```
  G              C     G
Bright  in  the  yellow  sun,

          D          G
There's  energy  for  everyone.

G              C     G
Bright  in  the  yellow  sun,

          D          G
Let  it  come,  let  it  come.
```

```
G                 C      G
Bright  in   the   yellow  sun,
                    D          G
There's  energy  for   everyone.
 G                  C      G
 Bright  in · the   yellow  sun,
                    D              G
Let  it   come,  let  it   come.
```

Verse 2:
```
     G    C      G
 Future  man  is   taking  steps,
 D                   G
 He  ain't  got  no  time  to  rest.
                     C     G                 C    G
 He's  the  future  man,    he's  the · future  man.
 G    C    G
 Future  lady's  getting  dressed,
 D                    G
 She's  gonna  clear  up   all  this  mess.
                     C     G  ·         D           G
 She's  the  future  lady,    she's  the  future  lady.
```

Chorus 2:
```
 G                        C      G
 The   wind  makes  the   windmill  turn,
           D                        G
 The  wind  makes  the  world  go  'round  and  'round
                         C      G
 The   wind  makes  the   windmill  turn,
           D                 G
 Let  it  blow,  let  it   blow!

 G                        C      G
 The   wind  makes  the   windmill  turn,
           D                        G
 The  wind  makes  the  world  go  'round  and  'round
                         C      G
 The   wind  makes  the   windmill  turn,
           D              G
 Let  it  blow,  let  it   blow!
```

Repeat Verse 1, Chorus 1, & Chorus 2:

THE WIND ENERGY SONG

Capo 2nd Fret
Starting Pitch: Open 2nd string

Words and Music by
MONTY HARPER

Standard Chords:

G

GITC Chords

G

Beginning Strum:

Intermediate Strum:

Verse 1:

G
This is the sun shining down on Earth.

Verse 2:

G
This is the warmth of the sun shining down on Earth.

Verse 3:

G
This is the air rising up through the warmth of the sun shining down on Earth.

Verse 4:

G
This is the wind blowing in beneath the air rising up through the warmth of the

Sun shining down on Earth.

Verse 5:

G
This is the rotor spinning in the wind blowing in beneath the

Air rising up through the warmth of the sun shining down on Earth.

Verse 6:

G
This is the generator running on the rotor spinning the wind blowing in beneath the

Air rising up through the warmth of the sun shining down on Earth.

Verse 7:

G
This is electricity flowing from the generator running on the rotor spinning in the

Wind blowing in beneath the air rising up through the

Warmth of the sun shining down on Earth.

Verse 8:

G

This is the light from the lamp I lit with electricity flowing from the

Generator running on the rotor spinning in the wind blowing in beneath the

Air rising up through the warmth of the sun shining down on Earth.

Verse 9:

G

This is the book I'm reading in the light from the lamp I lit with

Electricity flowing from the generator running on the

Rotor spinning in the wind blowing in beneath the air rising up through the

Warmth of the sun shining down on Earth.

Verse 10:

G

What is the title of the book I'm reading in the

Light from the lamp I lit with

Electricity flowing from the generator running on the

Rotor spinning in the wind blowing in beneath the air rising up through the

Warmth of the sun shining down on Earth?

Verse 11:

G

This is the Sun Shining Down on Earth is the

Title of the book I'm reading in the light from the lamp I lit with

Electricity flowing from the generator running on the rotor spinning in the

Wind blowing in beneath the air rising up through the

Warmth of the sun shining down on Earth.

Verse 12:

G
This is the sun shining down, shining down on Earth.

This is the sun shining down on Earth.

This is the sun shining down, shining down on Earth.

This is the sun shining down on Earth.

This is the sun shining down, shining down on Earth.

This is the sun shining down on Earth.

THE ELECTRIC CAR SONG

Capo 5th Fret
Starting Pitch: Open 2nd string

Words and Music by
NANCY SCHIMMEL

Standard Chords:

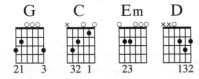

GITC Chords:

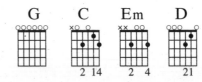

Beginning Strum:

Intermediate Strum:

Chorus:

G   C
Hybrids are better than regular cars,

   Em   D
A bicycle's cleaner than either.

G   C   Em
Walking is great when the trip isn't far,

          G   D G
Just dress yourself up for the weather.

Verse 1:

          C   G   C   G
In a regular car, when you step on the brakes,

   Em   D
The energy's wasted as heat, but a

C   G   C   G
Hybrid can store that a - way to use later, yeah.

Em   D
That's what makes hybrid's so neat.

Repeat Chorus:

Verse 2:

C   G   C G
When you plug in your eco - electric,

   Em   D
The energy may come from coal.

        C   G   C   G
And coal - fired plants are not clean enough

   Em   D
If clean is your car - driving goal.

Repeat Chorus:

Verse 3:

```
C       G     C                G
Electric cars  store  up   their  power
        Em                    D
In    batteries that  can   run   low.
        C           G            C        G
But   hybrids that  plug  in   switch  over   to   gas.
Em                  D
Anywhere you   desire,  hybrids  can   go.
```

Chorus:

```
G                        C
Hybrids are   better  than  regular  cars,
        Em                  D
A    bicycle's cleaner  than   either.
G                        C        Em
Walking is    great  when  the   trip   isn't  far,
        G                         D  G
Just   dress  yourself up   for   the   weather.
        G                           D  G   C   G   D   G
Just   dress  yourself up   for   the   weather.
```

SOLAR POWER'S IN

Capo 3rd Fret
Starting Pitch: Open 2nd string

Words and Music by
NANCY SCHIMMELL

Standard Chords:

GITC Chords:

Beginning Strum:

Intermediate Strum:

Advanced Strum:

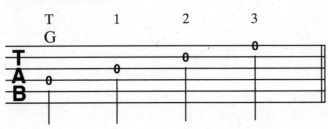

Verse 1:

G   C
Solar power's in your future,

G   D
Solar is for everyone.

G   C
In the night, we'll use the windmills,

G   D
In the day, we'll use the sun.

Chorus:

D   G   C
Oh, the sun is far away.

G   D
Close enough to light my day.

G   C   G
Close enough to warm my skin.

            D   G
Oh, let the sun shine in.

Verse 2:

```
    G                            C
    Here's  a   trick  they  do  with  mirrors,
    G                              D
    Don't  need  coal  to  make  a   fire.
    G                          C
    Bounce  the  sunlight  to  the  boiler,
    G                              D
    Send  the  power  on  the  wire.
```

Repeat Chorus:

Verse 3:

```
    G                          C
    You  don't  need  a   lot  of  money,
    G                              D
    You  just  need  the  sun  to  shine.
    G                        C
    Build  yourself  a   solar  oven,
    G                              D
    Dry  your  laundry  on  the  line.
```

Chorus:

```
    D      G           C
    Oh,  the  sun  is  far  away.

    G                            D
    Close  enough  to  light  my  day.
    G                  C          G
    Close  enough  to  warm  my  skin.
              D           G
    Oh,  let  the  sun  shine  in.
              D           G
    Oh,  let  the  sun  shine  in.
              D           G  C  G
    Oh,  let  that  sun  shine  in.
```

Chapter 9
Keep the Vision Alive!

Image Credit: NASA

by Yvonne de Villiers

A note of encouragement to students

I have taught ecology, been a stained glass artist and now design guitars. Many of my designs for both stained glass and guitars have been influenced by the Flora and Fauna (plants and animals) of this beautiful blue planet we are privileged to live on. I think it is important that each of us express our thoughts, and one of the ways to do so is through playing guitar and singing! Another way is by speaking and writing letters about things that matter. I am inspired to do what I do on the planet by YOU…the next generation.

We are all passengers on a beautiful blue spaceship we call "Earth," spinning at over 1000 miles per hour, and all the awesome plants and animals on the planet are also passengers spinning along with us. Imagine that! Like a regular spaceship, our living planet has a limited amount of precious air, water and food. Once it's gone, it's gone forever! So every personal decision we make to take care of our Earth, or not take care of her is of great importance.

If you were a passenger on a regular spaceship, would you ever think: "It doesn't matter if we pollute our water so we can't drink it"? Or "It doesn't matter if we don't take care of our garden and run out of food"? Or "It doesn't matter if we poison our air supply so we can't breathe it any more"? Of course not! You would take very good care of everything because your life, as well as the lives of all the other passengers would depend on it. We travel together like astronauts on this beautiful blue spaceship, dependent on its fragile supplies of air, soil and water. Like real astronauts, we must learn about and care for our blue spaceship to keep all its systems in balance.

An important thing you can do is KEEP ALIVE THE VISION of this big blue beautiful planet as a living thing. Take a good look at the picture at the beginning of this chapter. There are no real lines that divide states or countries or oceans. It is all one system. When birds fly through the air they see no boundaries. When fish swim in the oceans they see no boundaries. Boundaries that we think divide us by cities or states or countries are only man-made ideas. Water swirls around. Clouds swirl around. Wind swirls around. To take care of our earth, we need to think beyond boundaries. Small changes in one part of the world can have big effects in the rest of the world. There is a scientific theory called the Butterfly Effect that says that even the flapping of a butterfly's wings in Brazil can set off a tornado in Texas.

You might be thinking…but I'm just a kid! The world is so big! What can I do? The answer is simple: Anything you can. Everything matters, even the smallest thing! You can start by taking all the good ideas and information you have learned in this book and putting them into action in your life; even if it's just one thing every day. And share what you have learned with other people in your life. Ghandi once said "Whatever you do may seem insignificant, but it is most important that you do it."

To KEEP THE VISION ALIVE is to "think globally and act locally." What does this mean? It means keeping the vision of our earth as the blue spaceship that is our big home while doing what you can on the little spot where you live. Remember that small changes in one part of the world can have a big effect in the rest of the world. Be that small change! Be the Butterfly flapping its wings!

Look around you. Read or listen to the news. If you see something you disagree with that you think is bad for the earth…speak up! There are lots of ways to make your opinions known.

Can kids challenge things that adults are doing? Absolutely! It's YOUR future and your right as a citizen of this planet! And plants and animals don't have voices, so you are speaking for them too! Abraham Lincoln once said "He has the right to criticize, who has the heart to help."

If you want to be taken seriously in any part of your life, good communication is the best tool, and it is a tool you will use your whole life. Make sure you know your facts. Make sure you know what you want to say. And find out how to say it in a respectful way. When writing a good letter or speaking before a government body, there are rules you need to follow to be heard. Find out what they are and follow them. Some people get angry when they are speaking about something they care about, and that is understandable. But remember that speaking the truth calmly, clearly and firmly with love in your heart is more powerful.

How We Can Make A Difference

Ask your teachers, parents, or a trusted adult to help you to do any of the following things to express an opinion or idea you may have. You can find lots of good "how to" information online.

1. Write a letter to the editor of your local newspaper sharing your feelings.
    http://www.ehow.com/how_8921_write-letter-editor.html

2. Write a petition and get it signed by as many people as you can and present it.
    http://www.ehow.com/how_16629_write-petition.html

3. Write a complaint letter that gets results to a corporation. Many corporations try to look green on the surface, but it is sometimes a slimy shade of green. They may talk the talk, but don't walk the walk. Hold them accountable. http://www.ehow.com/how_2377405_register-complaint-big-company-heard.htm

4. Learn how to organize a peaceful protest. Talk to your police department about local regulations to make sure you are not trespassing.
    http://www.ehow.com/how_135670_organize-protest-march.html

5. Write a letter to your city council or attend a meeting. The more students the better. Involve your whole class or grade level. (Search the Internet for members names, address, local meeting dates and meeting rules for your local city council. Be sure you understand the proper way to address them when speaking.

6. Write a letter to your county commission or attend a meeting. Again, the more students the better. Involve your whole class or grade level. (As above, search the Internet information.)

7. Write a letter to the mayor of your city. Search the Internet under "contact mayor of [your town]."

8. Write a letter to your governor. Search the Internet under "contact governor of [your state]."

9. Write a letter to your senator. http://www.senate.gov/reference/common/faq/How_to_contact_senators.htm

10. Write a letter to your congressman/woman. https://writerep.house.gov/writerep/welcome.shtml

11. Write to the Supreme Court. http://usgovinfo.about.com/blsupct.htm

12. Write a letter to the President! http://www.whitehouse.gov/contact

13. Try to get your local paper or TV station to cover issues. If your class is going to show up at a city council meeting with a petition, or if you will be holding a peaceful protest, call your local newspaper and television channels. You will reach a lot more people this way that may also choose to be involved.

14. SING about what you care about. Write a song about what you want to say like the people who wrote the amazing songs in this book did! Three chords and the truth are powerful stuff and have the ability to move hearts and minds. So sing! Sing loud!!!!!!

15. Fly an Earth flag! - Fly one at your school or petition your city to fly one at city hall as a reminder to think globally while acting locally. http://www.earthflags.com/

Knowledge is Power: Where to Learn More

Books

- *The Lorax*, by Dr. Seuss
- *You Are the Earth*, by David Suzuki
- *You're Aboard Spaceship Earth*, by Patricia Lauber
- *National Geographic's True Green Kids: 100 Things You Can Do To Save The Planet* by Kim McKay and Jenny Bonnin, David De Rothschild
- *S is for Save the Planet: A How-To-Be Green Alphabet*, by Linda Holt Ayriss
- *You Can Save the Planet: 50 Ways You Can Make A Difference from Scholastic* by Jacquie Wines
- *Heroes of the Environment: True Stories of People Who Are Helping to Protect Our Planet*, Harriet Rohmer and Julie McLaughlin

Organizations

- The Hubble Telescope Site; http://www.hubblesite.org/
- Unicef; http://www.unicef.org/voy/explore/explore.php
- Kids Can Make A Difference; http://www.kidscanmakeadifference.org/what_kids_can_do.htm

Websites

- News and Information about the Sun-Earth Environment; www.spaceweather.com
- One Child's Voice Making a Difference; http://www.youtube.com/watch?v=EWxjzazIPjU
- Planet Save; http://planetsave.com/
- The Discovery Channel; http://dsc.discovery.com/tv/energy-365/
- TreeHugger; http://www.treehugger.com/files/2006/04/25_ways_to_save.php
- Flash Earth- Satellight and Aerial Imagery; http://www.flashearth.com/
- NASA TV; http://www.nasa.gov/multimedia/nasatv/index.html

Get a Little Help Writing Good Letters:

- http://usgovinfo.about.com/od/uscongress/a/letterscongress.htm
- http://www.wikihow.com/Write-a-Letter-to-the-Mayor-of-Your-City
- http://wiki.answers.com/Q/How_do_I_properly_address_a_letter_to_the_governor_of_a_state
- http://www.ehow.com/how_5666170_address-supreme-court-justice-correspondence.html

Find these and many more helpful website addresses at www.greensongbook.com.

MY RAINBOW RACE

Capo None
Starting Pitch: 4th fret, 1st string

Words and Music by
PETE SEEGER

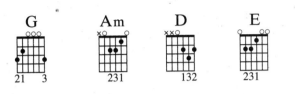
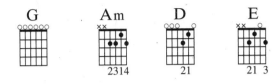

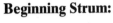

Beginning Strum:

Advanced Strum:

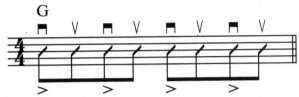
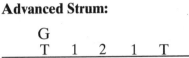
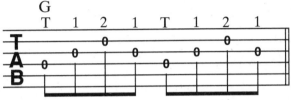

Chorus:

G   Am   D   G
One blue sky above us, one ocean lapping on our shore,

E   Am   D   G
One earth so green and round, who could ask for more?

G   Am   D   G
And because I love you, I'll give it one more try

E   Am   D   G
To show my rainbow race it's too soon to die.

Verse 1:

G   Am
Some folks want to be like an ostrich,

D   G
Bury their heads in the sand.

E   Am
Some hope that plastic dreams

             D   G
Can unclench all those greedy hands.

G   Am
Some hope to take the easy way:

D   G
Poisons, bombs. They think we need 'em.

E   Am
Don't you know you can't kill all the unbelievers?

         D   G
There's no shortcut to freedom.

114

Repeat Chorus:

Verse 2:

G   Am
Go tell, go tell all the little children.

D   G
Tell all the mothers and fathers too.

E   Am
Now's our last chance to learn to share

                    D   G
What's been given to me and you.

Chorus:

G   Am   D   G
One blue sky above us, one ocean lapping on our shore,

E   Am   D   G
One earth so green and round, who could ask for more?

G   Am   D   G
And because I love you, I'll give it one more try

E   Am   D   G
To show my rainbow race it's too soon to die.

Repeat Chorus two times

MAN IN THE MIRROR

Capo: None
Starting Pitch: Open 2nd string

Words and Music by
SIEDAH GARRETT and GLEN BALLARD

Standard Chords:

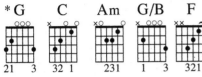

*The chords in this song go beyond the basic GITC chord fingerings.
Either use the standard tuning chords for this song,
or feel free to use the suggested, more advanced Open G tuning chords.

GITC Chords:

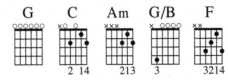

Beginning Strum:

Intermediate Strum:

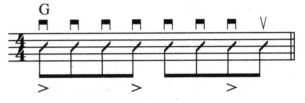

Verse 1:

    G   C
I'm gonna make a change for once in my life

                 G
It's gonna feel real good, gonna make a difference

                          C
Gonna make it right

               G
As I turn up the collar on my favorite winter coat
C
    This wind is blowin' my mind

               G
I see the kids in the street with not enough to eat

                C
Who am I to be blind, pretending not to see their needs

Bridge:

Am   G/B
A summer's disregard, a broken bottle top

C   G/B
And a one man's soul

          Am   G/B
They follow each other on the wind ya' know

                C   D
'Cause they got nowhere to go

                           G
That's why I want you to know

Chorus:

```
G   G/B                 C              D
I'm  starting with  the  man  in  the  mirror
G   G/B              C         D
I'm  asking  him  to  change  his  ways
G       G/B                   C
And  no  message  could  have  been  any  clearer
            F
If  you  wanna  make  the  world  a  better  place
                                                G
Take  a  look  at  yourself  and  then  make  a  change,     yey
                          C
Na  na  na,  na  na  na,  na  na  na  na  oh  ho
```

Verse 2:

```
G
I've  been  a  victim  of  a  selfish  kinda  love
C                                    G
   It's  time  that  I  realize  there  are  some  with  no  home

Not  a    nickel  to   loan.
               C
Could  it  be  really  me  pretending  that  they're  not  alone
```

Bridge:

```
Am                     G/B
A   willow  deeply  scarred,  somebody's  broken  heart
C                  G/B
And  a  washed  out  dream  (Washed  out  dream)
         Am                          G/B
They  follow  the  pattern  of  the  wind  ya'  see
                C              D
'Cause  they  got  no  place  to  be
                              G
That's  why  I'm  starting  with  me
```

Chorus:

```
G   G/B                 C              D
I'm  starting  with  the  man  in  the  mirror
G   G/B              C         D
I'm  asking  him  to  change  his  ways
G       G/B                   C
And  no  message  could  have  been  any  clearer
            F
If  you  wanna  make  the  world  a  better  place
                                                G
Take  a  look  at  yourself  and  then  make  a  change,     yey
```

```
G    G/B               C              D
I'm  starting  with  the  man  in  the  mirror

G    G/B               C              D
I'm  asking  him  to  change  his  ways

G        G/B               C
And  no  message  could  have  been  any  clearer

         F
If  you  wanna  make  the  world  a  better  place

                                              G
Take  a  look  at  yourself  and  then  make  a  change,    yey

G    G/B               C              D
I'm  starting  with  the  man  in  the  mirror

G    G/B               C              D
I'm  asking  him  to  change  his  ways

G        G/B               C
And  no  message  could  have  been  any  clearer
         F
If  you  wanna  make  the  world  a  better  place


Take  a  look  at  yourself  and  then  make  a  change


You  gotta  get  it  right,  while  you  got  the  time
                                              G
'Cause  when  you  close  your  heart  then  you  close  your  mind
```

Repeat Chorus:

WHAT A WONDERFUL WORLD

Capo 2nd Fret
Starting Pitch: open 3rd string

Words and Music by
GEORGE DAVID WEISS and BOB THIELE

Standard Chords:

G   Bm   C   D   B7   Em   Am7   D7

21   3   13421   32 1   132   213 4   23   2 1   213

GITC Chords:

G   Bm   C   B7   Em   Am7   D7

2341   2 13   12 4   2 4   2 1   21

Beginning Strum:

G

Advanced Strum:

G

3   3   3   3

Verse 1:

```
              G        Bm      C          G
I  see  trees  of  green,  red  roses  too,
C            G       B7         Em
I  see  them  bloom  for  me  and  you.
                  C
And  I   think  to   myself,
D7                    Em      C  D7
What  a   wonderful  world!
```

Verse 2:

```
              G      Bm       C         G
I  see  skies  of  blue  and  clouds  of   white,
        C          G
The   brightness  of  day,
        B7            Em
The   darkness  of  night,
                  C
And  I   think  to   myself,
D7                  G      C  G
What  a   wonderful  world!
```

Chorus:

```
        D7                        G
The   colors  of  the  rainbow,  so  pretty  in  the  sky,
        D7                        G
Are   also  on  the  faces  of  the  people  passing  by.
              C          G          Em           G
I  see  friends  shaking  hands,  saying,  "How  do  you  do?"
C          G    Am7        D7
They're  really  saying,  "I   love  you!"
```

Verse 3:

```
            G       Bm  C                   G
I   hear  babies  cry,  and  watch  them  grow,

C                   G    B7          Em
They'll  learn  much  more  than  we'll  know.

            C
And  I    think  to   myself,

D7                   G       C   G
What   a   wonderful  world!
```

Repeat Chorus:

Verse 4:

```
            G       Bm  C       G
I    see   trees  of   green, red  roses  too,

C            G    B7                  Em
I    see   them  bloom  for  me   and  for  you.

            C
And  I    think  to   myself,

D7                   G       C   G
What   a   wonderful   world!
```

About The Green Songbook Contributors

Caprice Potter

Caprice Potter is the Director of the award winning Life Lab Science at Gateway School in Santa Cruz, California where she teaches kindergarten through eighth grade science in a quarter acre garden classroom. Her program has garnered a Sustainability Award and is certified as a School Yard Habitat through the National Wildlife Federation. Ms. Potter has dedicated her life's work to providing children with opportunities to understand where their food comes and how to grow as well as prepare it for themselves and others. She states, "I want children to understand the science of sustainable farming and to become passionate stewards of the earth."

Jack Johnson

Jack Johnson, and his wife Kim, have spent the last seven years effecting change in their home state of Hawaii and worldwide through involvement in many social and environmental issues. Jack Johnson's tour production team is at the forefront of the green touring movement, effecting change at many levels in the industry. In 2005, Jack Johnson, along with his crew, MusicMatters and leading environmental scientists developed the EnviroRider, an environmental handbook presenting eco-friendly options and actions for the various components of tour production. For Johnson's 2010 world tour, his production team, with the support of Reverb, continued to pave the way in green touring practices. Tour trucks and coaches used sustainable biodiesel where possible to reduce CO_2 emissions. Fans used mass transportation and the *All At Once* ride share program. Tour merchandise was made from sustainable materials with a focus on reusables and renewables. The tour worked with local food producers to promote and provide locally grown and organic foods and waste reduction measures were expanded with on-site water refill stations along with bio-ware, composting and recycling. Any remaining CO_2 emissions from the tour were offset through support of a variety of carbon management projects.

100% of Jack Johnson's 2008 tour profits were used to establish the Johnson Ohana Charitable Foundation, an endowment founded by Jack and Kim Johnson to support environmental, art, and music education now and into the future. *The Green Songbook* has been developed in part with generous support from the Johnson Ohana Charitable Foundation.

Mark Rauscher

Mark grew up on the beaches of Florida where his love of the sea led him to a career in oceanography. He has worked for the Surfrider Foundation the past 10 years organizing coastal environmental campaigns throughout the U.S. In his position as Beach Campaign Manager, Mark works hard to protect the oceans, waves, and beaches for the enjoyment of all people.

Andrew C. Revkin

Andrew C. Revkin writes the Dot Earth blog for the op-ed pages of The New York Times and is Senior Fellow for Environmental Understanding at Pace University. He has written on climate change and other global environmental issues since the early 1980s. He is the author of books on the Amazon rain forest, global warming and the changing Arctic and has received journalism awards from numerous organizations, including the National Academy of Sciences, the American Association for the Advancement of Science, and Columbia University. Revkin has been awarded an honorary doctorate by Pace and a John Simon Guggenheim Fellowship. He lives in the Hudson Valley where, in spare moments, he is a performing songwriter and member of the roots band Uncle Wade.
http://www.nytimes/revkin
http://j.mp/RevNew

Yvone de Villiers

Yvonne de Villiers is the founder and designer for Luna Guitars. She is a second generation Florida native who has spent a good part of her life teaching ecology and fighting development along Florida's sensitive marshes and estuaries. Recently, de Villiers established Musicians on a Mission, an initiative created to assist players in coming together to reclaim our rightful heritage to a sane and healthy planet.
http://www.yvonnedevilliers.com
http://www.modernguitars.com/archives/003819.html

Steve Van Zandt

Steve is a graduate of UC Santa Barbara in Environmental Studies/Geography. He received a multiple subject teaching credential from San Francisco State University and an Administrative Credential from San Jose State University. Steve worked as a Naturalist at San Mateo Outdoor Education and at Exploring New Horizons. He also worked as a Naturalist at Youth Science Institute and as a Co-Director/Intern Coordinator at Hidden Villa. Steve was a co-manager for the Pigeon Point Youth Hostel. He has been a classroom teacher (for kindergarten, 3rd and 4th grade) and a Life Lab / ESL teacher (for K-7). He is a founding and active member of the Banana Slug String Band. He has three children: Nathan, 22, Colin, 19, and Skyler, 19. Steve enjoys music, writing, poetry, ping-pong, vegetarian/vegan cooking, surfing and swimming under waterfalls. Steve's nature name at outdoor education is "Solar Steve."
bananaslugstringband.com
http://www.smcoe.k12.ca.us/outdoored/index.html

About the Recording Team

John Kiehl
Executive Producer / Chief Engineer
John Kiehl, is the co-founder with Robert Cavicchio of Soundtrack Recording Studios in Boston and NYC—a recording studio that is now 32 years old active in all areas of audio post production: music, motion picture sound, television, and corporate communication. John has worn all the hats: bass player, composer, engineer, computer programmer, and is especially proud of his ability to connect his clients with just the right restaurant in New York City for their palate (and pocketbook). John is very active in developing software that creates digital environments for the creation of music in an attempt to give everyone the chance to enjoy the making of their own music. Currently John is on the steering committee of "Music As A Natural Resource," a United Nations initiative that fosters the use of music in attacking the social and economic problems challenging our world. Guitars In The Classroom is already an integral part of that initiative.

Jessica Anne Baron
Producer & Arranger / Vocals / Acoustic Guitar
Please see "About the Author" on page 123.
www.guitarsintheclassroom.org
www.jessicabaron.com

Chris Hills
Producer & Arranger / Vocals / Acoustic Guitar
Born and raised in Cambridge, England, Chris started playing guitar at age fifteen and has been performing, recording, composing and teaching professionally since 2003. He has worked with the Guitars in The Classroom program in New York since 2009. Chris has released material with UK Hip-Hop duo The Nextmen, and his songs also appear on compilations from the KPM/Musichouse library label.
www.myspace.com/tunesbychris

Eva Brooks
Vocals
Eva was brought up in a musical household in Harlem, New York, and has been a singer, pianist, songwriter and performer for most of her life. Currently she teaches early childhood education in New York City.

Marie Gabrielle
Vocals / Slide Guitar
Born and raised in New York City, Marie has toured the world as a musician and has worked and/or performed with notables such as: B.B. King, Wyclef Jean, Lucinda Williams, Taj Mahal and Dr. John. In 2006 she was voted one of the "Top New Independent Artists" by Performing Songwriter Magazine and has produced and performed original arrangements for film, television and Off-Broadway. She is the recipient of several corporate and national grants for her continued support of World, Roots, Blues and Independent Music and is a BMI songwriter, voting member of NARAS, attending member of the United Nations sponsored ICCC, and Co-Founder of the Mexican Children's Education Fund, which is a private organization that brings education through arts and music to gifted children and families in Mexico.

Frank Christian
Acoustic Guitar
Frank Christian is a consummate songwriting musician, renowned for his virtuosic guitar playing. With guitar roots ranging from traditional folk to acoustic blues, to big band guitar picking, Frank interweaves his music with lyrics that reveal a richness of illusion and metaphor, infused with irony and densely-textured imagery. His last album, *Mister So & So* was cited as one of the top ten albums of 1997 by the Boston Globe.

Julia Kim
Violin
Julia Kim has recorded and toured with the world music group, *Mondetta* and a range of African artists from *Blk Sonshine* and *Vusi Mahlasela* to *Tananas,* and many in between. She has opened in concert for Cesaria Evora, Salif Keita, and more. Julia is also a doctor who has helped hundreds of women in South Africa recover from physical and emotional suffering. Now she lives and works in New York City as a global HIV/AIDS and Development Policy Advisor at the United Nations (UNDP).

Thom Wolke with his daughters, Sonja and Anna
Vocals
Please see "About the Photographer" on page 123.

Jessica Finkelberg Silver
Vocals
Trained as an opera singer, Jessica Silver is an arts-oriented journeywoman, having held nearly every job in the performing arts field. For the last 15 years, she has focused on performing arts presenting, venue management and consulting. Jessica sings and lives in New York City with her husband, a cat and two French Bulldogs.

Ric Schnupp
Mix Engineer
Ric Schnupp is a recording and mixing engineer in the New York City area. He and his professional partner work together to provide custom music for commercials, films, TV shows, and recording artists. Ric is both humbled and honored to be among the first Emerging Talent Members of the Manhattan Producer's Alliance.
http://www.ricschnupp.com

Matt Stamm
Engineer
Matt Stamm is a singer, songwriter, session musician, and producer in New York. His songs have been placed in several films, television shows, and commercials, including NBC's Olympic coverage and the documentary FEAT: 63 Marathons in 63 Days. He released a new solo album in fall, 2010.
For more information, visit www.mattstamm.com.

Ben Arons
Engineer
Ben is a drummer, audio engineer and photographer. He freelances as a drummer and currently plays with the Broadway-bound musical hit, *Bloody Bloody Andrew Jackson*. Recording and mixing projects include work with Russell Simins of the Jon Spencer Blues Explosion, Karen O of the Yeah, Yeah, Yeahs, Harper Simon, NBC, CBS and Jimmy Fallon (The Bathroom Wall). His photos have appeared in The Village Voice, Drumhead and CMJ magazines.
www.benaronsphoto.com

About the Book Makers

Dick Boak
Cover artist
http://www.dickboak.com/

Dick Boak nearly lost his eyesight at the age of six and ever since, has concerned himself with visual details. Unable to surpass his older brothers in the sports arena, he focused instead on drawing, woodworking, writing and music. In his teens, he self-published two booklets of poetry, immersed himself in technical drafting, and began to experiment with musical instrument design and construction. Fascinated with the architecture of Buckminster Fuller, he began designing and building geodesic domes. Following a pragmatic yet artistic path combining building, art and design, Dick spent his most artistically prolific years as a conceptual illustrator, later becoming an art teacher, lathe turner, performing musician and luthier. In 1973, he came to work at C. F. Martin & Co. as a design draftsman. Since then and for the past 32 years, he has held many diverse and creative positions there, forming Martin's Artist Relations Department and the conception of more than one hundred and forty signature guitar collaborations with the top musical talents of our time. His acclaimed book *Martin Guitar Masterpieces* relays the stories of those collaborations. Currently living in Nazareth, Pennsylvania with his wife Susan and their two daughters Emily and Grace, he continues to build his legacy with The Martin Guitar Company, finding occasional time to further his art and music, and work on the publication of his more personal book *Dot To Dot—The Creative, Comical & Covert Adventures of Dick Boak*. The artwork for the cover of *The Green Songbook* is the first illustration that Dick has done in fifteen years since losing sight in one eye. As a friend to GITC, he honored the organization's special request for his participation.

Nancy Schimmel
Content Consultant

Nancy Schimmel was a children's librarian in the sixties, then set out on her own as a storyteller. She wrote one of her first songs for the first Earth Day in 1970, and has been writing and performing ever since. Nancy's albums have won Parent's Choice™ and American Library Association awards. She is a member of the Children's Music Network. Nancy has recorded three CDs with Candy Forest and Fran Avni, which are available at Nancy's website, www.sisterschoice.com.

Aaron Stang
Book Supervisor, Musical Director

Aaron Stang is the lead author on the *Guitar Expressions* project. He is also the author of Alfred Music Publishing's *21st Century Guitar Method*, one of the most popular guitar methods in publication, which has been translated into Spanish, French, German, and Japanese. Aaron is a feature artist on the Grammy award-winning CD, Henry Mancini, *Pink Guitar* (Solid Air Records). *Pink Guitar* won the Grammy for the "Best Pop Instrumental Album" at the 47th Annual Grammy Awards. Aaron is an acquisition editor for Alfred Music Publishing and has overseen the publication of hundreds of books and videos. Aaron performs solo and with his group, Relative Viewpoint, in concerts and folk festivals throughout South Florida.

Karen Farnum Surmani
Editor

Karen Farnum Surmani is the Early Childhood and Vocal Masterworks Acquisition Editor for Alfred Music Publishing, and is the author of *Teach Yourself to Sing* and *Singing 101*. She is a co-author of *Rock Singing Techniques*, *Alfred's Essentials of Music Theory*, *Sing at First Sight*, and *Classroom Music for Little Mozarts*. Karen received a Bachelor of Music degree in Vocal Performance from California State University, Northridge and a Masters in Music Education degree from the University of Southern California. She is a credentialed elementary and Orff-certified music teacher and also has extensive training in early childhood music education. An accomplished classical vocalist, Karen sings professionally and teaches private voice. As a result of *The Green Songbook*, she is now happily taking guitar lessons.

Eric Kalver
Production Editor

Eric is the Choral and Early Childhood Production Editor for Alfred Music Publishing. He is a Magna Cum Laude and Dean's List graduate of Berklee College of Music in Boston, MA, holding Bachelor of Music degrees in Contemporary Writing & Production and Percussion Performance. Eric obtained much arranging and copyist experience in recent years including his association with film/TV composers James Sale and Brian Tyler, and as an orchestrator on the Universal Studios motion picture, *Skyline*, which was released in November 2010. Eric works as a freelance drummer, composer, arranger, and copyist in the Los Angeles area.

Matt Koprowski
Layout/Graphic Designer

Matt Koprowski is a graphic designer at Alfred Music Publishing. He graduated from California State University, Northridge with a Bachelor of Arts degree in Music Industry Studies.

Andrew Surmani
Marketing

Andrew Surmani is the Senior Vice President of Marketing and Managing Director, School and Church Publishing at Alfred Music Publishing. He is a co-author of *Alfred's Essentials of Music Theory* series. In addition to his Alfred duties, Andrew is a freelance musician in the Los Angeles area and teaches trumpet privately. Andrew also serves on the Executive Committee as President Elect for the Jazz Education Network (JEN), is on the Curriculum Committee for the CSUN Masters in Music Industry Studies degree program, the Music Technology Advisory Board at Indiana University - IUPUI, and is Founder and President of the MATES Foundation, a 501(c)(3) non-profit corporation formed to support a new arts and technology charter school in Thousand Oaks, California. Andrew has a Bachelor of Music degree in Trumpet Performance and an MBA from California State University, Northridge.

Nick Sinutko
Production Assistant: Guitars in the Classroom

Nick Sinutko is a 22 year-old self-taught musician from Northern and Southern California. He currently serves as Operations Director for Guitars in the Classroom, managing organizational projects and logistics, web development, and outreach. Nick's nature-heavy upbringing, and his time spent on Native American reservations have taught him that nothing could be more important than deepening our understanding of how we can live in harmony with the earth.

About the Author

Jessica Anne Baron, M.A.

Jessica Anne Baron founded and serves as Executive Director for Guitars in the Classroom, an organization that brings music making to education by integrating singing, strumming and songwriting with learning throughout the school day and across the curriculum. Jessica created the first developmental guitar instruction method and she has written six groundbreaking books in the field of music education. She passionately believes that we are all unique musical beings with individual pathways we must find and follow to learn to make music. Jess spent years in California teaching music in schools and working as a human development educator and educational therapist after receiving her Masters degree in Clinical Psychology from Antioch University. That study combined with a fascination with how we learn prepared her to create musical programs and curricula that help people become more whole, healthy, and creative. She co-authored the highly successful *MusicMakers* curriculum for the Boys and Girls Clubs of America, the International House of Blues Foundation's *Make an Impression* guitar program, and her best-selling guitar method, *SmartStart Guitar* as well as her parenting book, *YOUR MUSICAL CHILD: Inspiring Kids to Play and Sing for Keeps. The Green Songbook* marks her seventh, and Guitars in the Classroom's first official publication. Jess lives in Encinitas, California with her son, Eli, and a whole bunch of birds, two lizards, and a shih tzu named Homer. She enjoys eating rocky road ice cream, lying in the grass, singing songs of praise and real life, and hanging out with kids and teachers. She hopes you really love this book.

About the Photographer

Thom Wolke

Thom Wolke is a freelance photographer specializing in the entertainment industry and ecological portraiture. His work has appeared in Billboard, Downbeat, Dirty Linen, and Us magazines among others, and in newspapers, books, ecological and other publications nationally and internationally. Thom's work as an artist manager, concert promoter, and event coordinator aligns with his personal commitment to creating a healthy, sustainable environment through social awareness, action, and education. He generously volunteers with Guitars in the Classroom.

To see color versions of Thom's photographs used in this book, please visit www.thomwolkephotography.com. Sale of prints of any of these photographs will benefit Guitars in the Classroom.

Photo Credits

All photographs in this book represent the work of Thom Wolke, except biography photos, and those otherwise credited and the photos that accompany these pages:

- Jack in classroom (p. 3) – photograph by Steve Barilotti
- "Country Roads" (p. 24) – photograph by Anna Wolke
- "My Own Two Hands" (p. 23) – photograph by Kim Johnson
- "This Land is Your Land" (p. 27) – photograph by Gavin Mills (www.sxc.hu)
- "Talk of the Town" (p. 32)– photograph by Jessica Anne Baron
- "Healthy Habitats" (p. 39)– photograph by Sonja Wolke
- "Dolphins, Dolphins" (p. 68)– photograph by Amy J. Putnam
- "Someone's Gonna Use it After You" (p. 96)– photograph by Jessica Anne Baron

To receive more songs and information from Guitars in the Classroom, get up to date Green info, and to share your thoughts with other Green teachers and classrooms, please visit www.greensongbook.com.

Note for Pianists, Guitarists and Other Instrumentalists:

All of the songs in this book are arranged in the key of "G." This helps beginners play the song on guitar with only a few simple chord fingerings. Guitarists will use a capo to place the songs in the recorded keys and also to place them in comfortable keys for their own vocal range. However, pianists will have to transpose these songs and some guitarists may prefer to play them in their "sounding" keys without a capo. You can use the chart below to transpose these songs to any key you like.

To transpose, choose your key from the left column. The chords used in the book are listed across the top. For example, in the key of C#, the G chord becomes C#, the C chord becomes F#, and so on.

CHORDS USED IN BOOK

KEY	G	C	D	Am	Em	F
G	G	C	D	Am	Em	F
A♭	A♭	D♭	E♭	B♭m	Fm	G♭
A	A	D	E	Bm	F#m	G
B♭	B♭	E♭	F	Cm	Gm	A♭
B	B	E	F#	C#m	G#m	A
C	C	F	G	Dm	Am	B♭
C#	C#	F#	G#	D#m	A#m	B
D	D	G	A	Em	Bm	C
E♭	E♭	A♭	B♭	Fm	Cm	D♭
E	E	A	B	F#m	C#m	D
F	F	B♭	C	Gm	Dm	E♭
F#	F#	B	C#	G#m	D#m	E
	I	IV	V	IIm	Vim	♭VII

Index of Songs